Colin McEvedy The Penguin Atlas of Medieval History

Maps devised by the author
and drawn by John Woodcock

Penguin Books

INTRODUCTION

1 · *The Area Covered*

My idea in compiling this atlas has been to show the unfolding of medieval history in Europe and the Near East as a continuous story, an aim in contrast to that of most historical atlases, which illustrate discrete fragments of history and are intended primarily as works of reference. That the nations within this area have much history in common is an obvious fact which the purely national approach often ignores and the modern tendency for microscopic analysis tends to keep permanently out of focus. It is continually emphasized by the method of presentation here adopted and, if the result is at first sight a mere pictorial catalogue, a perspective emerges from the whole which establishes the relative proportions of different historical events.

There is no *geographical* detail on the maps – for example, the only English town shown is London – nor any dissection of political units – the Kingdom of France is simply the Kingdom of France and is never subdivided into Duchies, Counties, and so on. There is, however, much more chronological detail than is usual, each state being shown at many different points in time, and this, together with the constant scale, allows different epochs to be directly compared.

The thirty-eight maps that make up the atlas are arranged in five sections. The bulk of each section is made up of five or six maps showing the political state of the area at intervals that average forty years. Two more maps (indicated by the letters R and E after the date at the beginning of the text), corresponding in date to the last political one and showing respectively the extent of Christendom and the development of the economy, complete

the section. All the maps cover exactly the same area: Europe, North Africa, and the Middle East; the reasons for the choice of this area are fundamental to the whole atlas and require explanation at some length.

In the medieval period, the nations of Europe and the Near East formed a community, the members of which constantly reacted on each other but were almost completely cut off from the rest of the world by physical barriers. We can think of the Europe–Near-East area as a cul-de-sac, the rough outline of the sack being formed by the Arctic circle, Atlantic Ocean, and Sahara Desert (Figure 1). The southern limit can be carried around to the Arabian Sea and the lips of the sack drawn close together by bringing the upper down along the line of the Ural Mountains and the lower up the Suleiman Range. The mouth is thus reduced to the region of the Oxus and Jaxartes rivers (Russian Turkestan), and it can be said that all significant contacts between the Europe–Near-East area and the rest of the world took place via Turkestan. The apparent exceptions to this rule, the Norse, the Portuguese, and the Arab traders of the Saharan and spice routes, however stirring their individual sagas, never succeed in enlarging the European–Near-Eastern horizon during the period under consideration (360–1478).

A résumé of their achievements clearly demonstrates this. In the Atlantic the Norse discovered and colonized Greenland during the ninth century and they later reconnoitered a debatable amount of the coast of North America, which they termed Vinland, but these events were reported barely if at all in Europe, and the harsh conditions that eventually extinguished the Greenland colony did not encourage interest. The resources required for the sustained effort needed to breach the Atlantic barrier permanently were not in fact available until the fifteenth century, and the successful expedi-

tions of the 1490s lie outside our period. The discoveries made by the Portuguese before 1478 were relatively speaking unimportant – the Azores and the Atlantic coast of Africa as far as the Gulf of Guinea. The southern barrier, the Sahara, was not as formidable to the desert-bred Arab as it had been to the Romans, and shortly after the Islamic conquest of North Africa routes were opened up between Morocco–Algeria and the western Sudan, whose slaves, ivory, and gold provided the basis for a flourishing trans-Saharan trade. The contact between the two communities broadened briefly when the Murabits of Morocco turned south, shattered the Negro Empire of Ghana which had held much of the Niger and Senegal basins since the fourth century, and began the conversion of the population to Islam. After that, the link between the two communities became purely economic again and the native Islamic empire of Malli which replaced Ghana in 1240 pursued its history in effective isolation. To the east the spice route connecting India with Persia,

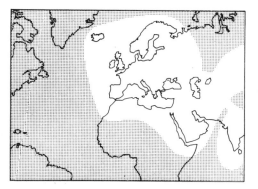

FIG. 1 The European–Near-Eastern community in medieval times, with the Indian and Central Asiatic (Nomadic) communities abutting it.

Arabia, and Egypt carried a far greater traffic than the Saharan route, but it also was responsible for the mediation of a politico-religious change on only one occasion. In 711, the Arabs sailed to Sind, the westernmost province of India and seized it for the Caliphate. Again the attempt to defy geography was only momentarily successful, and Sind, though effectively Islamized, was neither conscious of the temporal authority of the Caliph nor even remembered in Baghdad.

Granted that these incidents do not invalidate the essential circumscription of the Europe–Near-East area, there remains the mouth of the sack, Turkestan, where the settled agricultural communities of the Near East petered out and the Asiatic steppe, the domain of the nomad, began. The Indian cul-de-sac also opened on to western Turkestan (via the Khyber pass) and in antiquity,

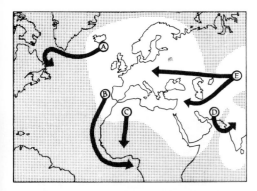

FIG. 2 Movements into and out of the European–Near-Eastern area

A: Norse (ninth–tenth centuries)
B: Portuguese (fifteenth century)
C: Murabits (thirteenth century)
D: Arabs (eighth century)
E: Nomads (throughout the period).

when the nearer parts of Turkestan were more definitely settled and could be counted within the Near-Eastern area, it was possible for the Persian and Macedonian empires to include an Indian province. During the medieval period, when the nomads' hold on Turkestan was unbroken, the land route to India was never attempted by a western army. The third settled civilization, the Chinese, lay on the other side of the screen of nomads, far beyond the effective political reach of the times. Overland trade between the civilized three was considerable, especially when the nomads erected their larger empires and the caravans could journey in safety, but, as with the Saharan and spice routes, communications were really too tenuous to bear anything weightier than luxuries and gospels; the nomads effectively tied the mouth of the sack.

If the nomads had been content with a static role, there could be no objection to the treatment of the Europe–Near-East area as an isolated entity; unfortunately their part was far from passive, and their aggressions brought a common factor into the history of China, India, Europe, and the Near East. Huns, Turks, and Mongols are part of the story of each. The Near East and India, sharing adjacent openings on to Asia, often shared the same storm from the Steppe; the power of the Kushans, White Huns, and Timurids for example, originally centered on the Oxus basin, extended simultaneously into the Near East, Asia proper, and India; and though China was further away, the exceptional empire – the Turkish in the sixth century and the Mongol in the thirteenth – could bear on both China and the Europe–Near-East area at the same time. But if there is an intrusive element in the history of all three, India, China, and the Europe–Near-Eastern powers could only affect each other indirectly by some effort against the interposed nomads (for example,

Chinese attacks weakened the Turkish Khanate in the seventh century and thus eased the Arab conquest of Transoxiana), and as long as notice is taken of the doings of the nomads in Turkestan and of their Chinese and Indian interests the Europe–Near-East area can I think be fairly considered in vacuo.

The area within the sack as defined in Figure 1 contains a lot of dead space; the area taken as the base map for this book (it is superimposed on the first in Figure 3) eliminates most of this. On the northern and western borders the sacrifice of northern Scandinavia, Iceland, the Canaries, and the Atlantic coast of Africa allows a great reduction in area without more than insignificantly affecting the historical comprehensiveness of the map. A more drastic economy has been made in the south – the exclusion of the Eastern Sudan, Abyssinia, and the southern third of the Arabian peninsula. Nubia and Abyssinia are natural backwaters and, in the medieval period, they were further isolated by their Christian faith, which made them alien to their Moslem neighbours. The petty Nubian principalities were finally destroyed by the Mamluks in the thirteenth and fourteenth centuries; Abyssinia lost her coastline to the Arabs in the tenth century but was otherwise left alone. The Arabs colonized the coast as far south as Zanzibar during the tenth and twelfth centuries but never reached or knew of Madagascar. (Below Zanzibar, the southward current was considered too fast to allow a return journey.) To leave out such areas is reasonable enough. The Kingdoms of South Arabia, staging posts on the limb of the spice route that went to Egypt and East Africa, are also little loss, for the desert effectively cut them off from the other Middle-Eastern countries. But from the desert itself came one of the most vital of medieval forces, Islam. The exclusion of part of its birthplace is justified by the attitude of Islam itself, no more tied to Arabia than Christianity to Palestine. Within thirty years of the Prophet's death, Arabia had become a mere province of the Empire of Damascus, and it then reverted to its original conditions of unorganized nomadism. The Islamic powers were neither interested in the affairs of such a desolate border territory nor, except in so far as they concerned the Mecca pilgrimage route, aware of them. Under the circumstances two thirds of Arabia really seems quite enough.

The eastern border cuts off some of Persia in the south and, because of the exigencies of the projection, includes an unnecessary part of Siberia in the north. The excluded part of Persia is mostly desert and plays a passive role in history, nearly always as a province of the state controlling the parts visible on the map. The middle section of the eastern border extends beyond the upper and lower part to show the Turkestanian neck; the name in the overlap is thus that of the temporary stopper of the European–Near-Eastern bottle.

2 · The Shadings Used

In the political maps the language of the dominant people in any state can be deduced from the shading of the state or the type of border around it. A classification by language is at first sight a poor substitute for the real requirement, a classification by race. This ideal has not been attempted, partly because so far no system based on physical characteristics has progressed much beyond the white–brown–yellow–black division of common observation. The apparently more scientific investigations, such as skull measurement and blood group determination, are only of real use in the study of small isolated populations and tend to

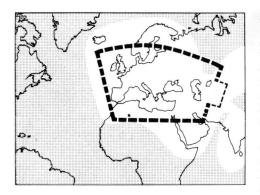

FIG. 3 The area covered by the base map used in this book.

give the same answer each time when applied to larger groups within the white race, the only one with which we are concerned. For that matter, anyone who in this day and age goes around measuring heads in the expectation of broadly applicable results invites a similar investigation, for, leaving apart the fact that skull shape is by no means entirely genetically determined, it is obvious that the concept of originally 'pure' races miscegenated by movements taking place in historic times is as obsolete as it is ancient. It must be replaced, as has the related doctrine of special creation of animal species, by a theory of continuous evolution. A pure race in such a view is simply one which has been isolated for sufficient time for a number of special characteristics to develop and within which there is the continual mixing necessary to spread these characteristics evenly throughout the population. But during any isolation more useful peculiarities than the merely physiognomical will appear: dialects progress in time to new languages and a small variation in the

pattern of a cooking-pot can be the first step toward a new culture. These changes of language and behaviour are susceptible to a far more rewarding analysis, for they give an indication of the ancestry of a group as well as a very sensitive index of its peculiarity. Bearing in mind that language, race, and culture are a single complex, the linguistic classification will be seen to be as valid as, and far more useful than, the purely physical.

By the late fourth century the inhabitants of the Roman Empire were predominantly Latin-speaking in the west, Greek-speaking in the east. Beyond the frontiers were 'barbarians' with languages belonging either to the Indo–European group to which both Latin and Greek belong, or to one of the other 'White' language groups, Hamito–Semitic (North African–Arabian) and Ural–Altaic (Asian). The languages of importance at the beginning of the medieval period are shown, together with their characteristic shadings or borders, in the larger circles in the map on the opposite page, which is the linguistic key for the atlas. Among the Indo–European tongues, Latin and Greek are left plain, Celtic is vertically lined, Teutonic given a dotted periphery, Slav and Balt diagonally lined in opposite senses, and Iranian horizontally lined. Within the Iranian group, Alans and Kurds are closely shaded, Persians broadly; the Armenians display a very close version of the Iranian type (see Map 362), for, although linguistically they deserve a pattern of their own, they were ethnically strongly Iranized and their aristocracy was entirely Persian. History has never been fair to the Armenians and it is too late to start being so now. The Hamites and Semites, for the purpose of this book synonymous with Berbers and Arabs, are cross-hatched, the Semites having the wider mesh. The Altaic Mongols and Turks have a border of circles, solid in one case, open in the other; the Uralian

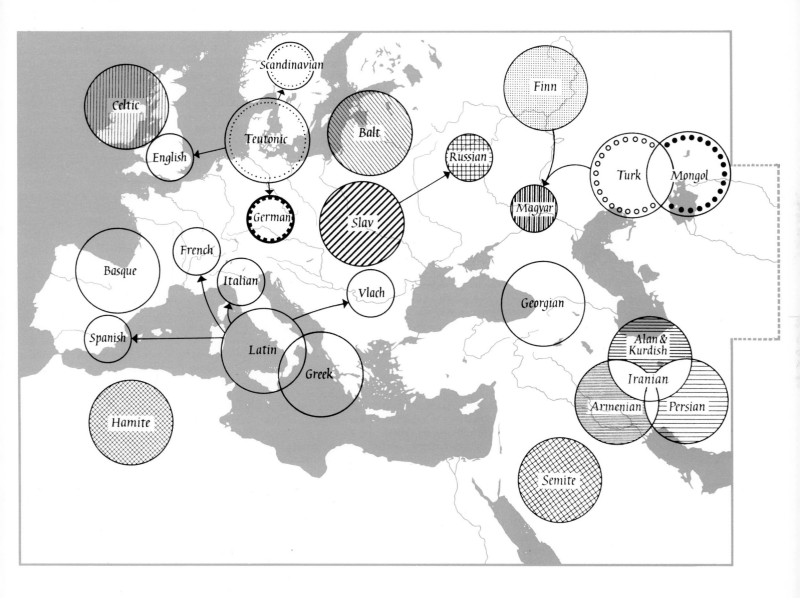

Finns are stippled. It is not known which of the Altaic languages was spoken by the Huns, and the choice of the Mongol rather than the Turkish symbol in their case (see Map 362) is entirely arbitrary.

The ethnic structure of the Roman Empire is a matter of Ancient History and, as by the language test each half was effectively homogenized in the fourth century, no dissection is undertaken here. But in some provinces the people did resist the assimilation process – one example is Britain, which remained Celtic-speaking to the end of the Empire; another is the region of the western Pyrenees, where the Basques clung to their native tongue, as indeed they still do today. Basque is believed to be related to the Georgian languages of Transcaucasia, which are equally non-Indo-European and unclassifiable; if it is, the two peoples may be the remnants of a once widespread population – a fourth 'White' language group – whose decline antedates our earliest records. The Basques, who make their first appearance on Map 476, have a great respect for their own antiquity, saying that when God needed some bones with which to make the first man, He took them from a Basque cemetery, and it would require a striking pattern to do justice to their oddity. But like the Georgians, present on Map 362 as the free tribes of Abasgians and the Kingdoms of Iberia and Lazica, they played only a minor role in medieval history so, rather than overstress their importance, I have left them plain.

The smaller circles in the map on p. 5 show the patterns used for languages which differentiated during the course of the period covered by the atlas. Spanish appears after the fall of Visigothic Spain (Map 737), French and Italian after the collapse of the Frankish Empire (Map 888), and Vlach in the fourteenth century (Map 1360), all these being Latin-derived languages and therefore unshaded. After Map 998 the continental Germans are all enclosed within the castellated border of their medieval Empire and dots became the distinguishing mark of the Scandinavians. The Normans lose these dots as they are assimilated, but for diagrammatic reasons the English do not regain theirs even when they have absorbed their French aristocracy; the evolution of Teutons (dots) into English (plain), Scandinavian (dots), and Germans (castellated) therefore lacks all visual logic. Similarly when the Magyars appear (Map 737) there is no sign of their parentage – basically Finnish with a Turkish element added – in their pattern of vertical stripes, and the Russians, when the time comes to differentiate them from the other Slavs (Map 998), are given a completely new pattern, and not one evolved from the Slavs oblique shading. In both cases the choice of a contrasting symbol has been dictated by the desire to maintain the clarity of the maps at a time when the history is getting increasingly complicated. As a last inconsistency the dotted border is also used for the crusader states, Baltic, Levantine, and Aegean; although Teutons monopolized the Baltic crusades, those in the Mediterranean were dominated by the French and Normans and the use of dots cannot be justified ethnically or linguistically. The crusader states needed a unifying characteristic however, and dots provide a satisfactory echo of the *Völkerwanderung* of the fifth and sixth centuries.

Besides giving an overall linguistic picture and the division into states, the maps also indicate in an approximate manner the degree to which the various political entities were internally organized. At the tribal level there is no bounding line around the shading, and only when the tribe evolves a stable Kingship is it given an outline; if it becomes an Empire the line is thickened. The exceptions to this rule are the Scandinavian Kingdoms, which are never outlined.

For Kingdoms it would have been useful to give both the dynasty and the country ('Norman Kingdom of England') or, in the case of Islamic dynasties, which are usually coupled with their capital, the name of this as well as the dynastic title ('Umayyad Emirate of Cordova'). Considerations of space prohibit the use of these full titles, and I have named the western Kingdoms of early days by their founder tribes, and, after the fall of the Frankish Empire, by their country (Frankish Kingdom, Kingdom of France). The eastern states are referred to simply by dynasty except when a dynasty has several branches, in which case they are distinguished by their capital towns (Buwahids of Baghdad, Hamadan, and Isfahan).

The names of the Turco–Mongol dynasties seem to cause more difficulty than can be explained by their exotic spelling and pronunciation. The important point to remember is that a dynasty, such as the Seljuk, must be distinguished from a people, such as the Ghuzz, just as the Hohenstaufen must be distinguished from the Germans. In the transliteration of Islamic and Turco–Mongol names I have been eclectic, trying to follow in the majority of cases the versions favoured by modern scholars, but retaining inconsistencies hallowed by time. For instance I have allowed Murabit and Muwahid to replace Almoravid and Almohad but retained Ottoman and Ghuzz in place of the more exact forms Osmanli and Toquz-oghuz. In the case of linguistic groups with a distinctive shading, the names are omitted after a few appearances.

3 · Limitations

The reader of any historical atlas should be warned against allowing his critical faculties to be disarmed by the apparent objectivity of a map. The shape of a coastline, the site of a town, these are facts and subconsciously influence us into accepting as true other matter which is in fact presented in a highly subjective manner. The thickness of a line, the sizes of lettering, etc., all emphasize certain features of what is, really, part map and part picture. I had hoped to keep opinion confined to the commentary accompanying these maps, but I must admit that this has been impossible. The best I can claim is that the uncertainties posed have been resolved in the maps with the maximum objectivity I can command. There has, of course, been no attempt to keep opinion out of the commentary, in fact although there is no wilfully unfair selection of facts, at times one can perhaps discern the subtle bouquet of prejudice.

The varying length of time that separates each map is an obvious example of the type of treatment that can easily progress to partiality. It would be best to have maps at fixed intervals and not to be swayed into compressing or extending the interval by a desire to show an Empire at its absolute peak or a situation at its most critical. However, to keep a fixed interval and yet tell the story of the Middle Ages would require a large number of maps, possibly three times as many here. The unequal distribution I have adopted is simply a consequence of the need to economize.

In the case of vassal states, no method of treatment could claim to be exact, for there is a series of possible positions that shade into one another. A vassal can effectively be the province of the larger state with only a nominal autonomy or be in fact independent, merely recognizing the formal suzerainty of an impotent monarch. It may pay only a token amount of tribute and yet consider itself a part of the larger whole, while on the other hand a defeated state may be paying a crushing blackmail without surrendering any of its sovereignty. In such cases, whether to show a state as independent or as a vassal or to incorporate it within an Empire without distinguishing it at all must be a personal decision with which others might easily disagree. A special border ($\cdots - \cdots -$) is used for fiefs held by one sovereign power within the territory of another (for example by the King of England within France) or for those held by a non-sovereign power with lands in more than one state (for example the Duke of Burgundy with lands in both France and Germany). No other fiefs are shown.

Even in the apparently factual reporting, there are debatable points, for medieval history as a study is not without its controversies. Where the borders are uncertain, or, as is even more often the case, were never more than extremely vague, I have tried to indicate this by keeping them geometrically simple. Compared to the majestic lacunae in our knowledge of medieval economics, however, the political uncertainties are few and far between, and in the series of maps dealing with the economy of the Europe–Near-East area much of the information presented is suppositious in the extreme. So that the pattern of urbanization can be seen, only towns of a certain size are shown. A simple black circle represents a town with a minimum of twenty-five thousand inhabitants, the addition of an outer ring to the circle shows that the number of inhabitants is at least three times the minimum, i.e. a seventy-five thousand or more. So far so good; but unfortunately the data required is almost entirely lacking. The final result rests on a few facts, a deal of assumption, and frankly a deal more guess-work. In most cases the size of a town's population in medieval times can only be a matter of opinion. However, with more confidence than I would have in argument over a particular town, I can say that I believe the overall picture to be sufficiently true to justify the scheme.

4 · Background Notes

The medieval period opened with the fall of the Mediterranean Empire of Rome in the West and its replacement by a new superficially Germanized society, which gradually evolved the feudal state. With the slow conquest of the Eastern half of the Empire by Islam, which also overran the African provinces of the West, and with the integration of the Slavs into Christendom, the emphasis in the Christian world shifted northwards. Thus at the end of the Middle Ages, while the Latin (Catholic) Church easily outshone the Greek (Orthodox), both were confined to continental Europe. A string of Islamic nations ringed the Mediterranean, their bulk appearing to prevent Christendom from ever expanding again in spite of an increasing Christian preponderance in wealth and technology.

At intervals throughout the ten centuries that separate the sack of Rome from that of Constantinople, waves of nomads appeared from Asia to terrorize their enemies, the agriculturalists and town dwellers. Their devastations did much to undermine the prosperity of Islam and to prevent Russia from developing in step with the rest of Europe, but by the end of the period they were clearly the losing side.

Many subjects deserve fuller discussion than can be given in the commentaries that accompany the maps, but in this brief summary of the Middle Ages three subjects in particular demand additional treatment. Without some understanding of the fall of the Western Roman Empire, the evolution and decay of feudal society, and the recurrent nomadic invasions, the course of medieval history would appear erratic and meaningless.

THE FALL OF ROME

The final end of the classical world is a subject which for most people has a tragic aspect and this reaction is worth some analysis. Both the sheer size of the Empire, never equalled in the West before or since, and the many characteristics, absent in the Dark Ages, which our civilization shares with the Roman in the fields of culture, law, and administration, contribute to this feeling. But were the victories of the Germans really a disaster for mankind? Such a view is best examined by considering what would have happened if the Empire had survived – by considering China, for example, where, although individual Empires existed only for a span, it was fundamentally the same Empire that was recreated each time. The result was a tendency to stagnation or at least the mere reshuffling of elements that had been created in the early days of Chinese history. The concept of a few eternal verities may be attractive, but there is a lot to be said for searching for new truths even at the expense of the old. Rome had given all it had to give, and, though considerable flexibility was still exhibited in some ways, late Roman society lacked vitality. At the end, the talents were not multiplying, they were simply buried.

This brings us to a problem that can be considered in more concrete terms; why did the Western Empire fall when it did? The immediate answer is, of course, the advance of the Huns, which frightened the Germans into doing what they had long had the capacity to do, for both in numbers and in arms they were by then superior to the legionaries who manned the frontiers. The decline in the Empire's total population may have been absolute or merely comparative to barbarian increase. It may have been due to the fact that a sizeable proportion of the masses were slaves (slaves had a notoriously low reproduction rate), or to a high death rate in the urban proletariat, which must have been decimated by endemic and epidemic diseases. But whatever the extent or the reason, the manpower situation of the Empire certainly deteriorated vis-à-vis the German, and this deterioration was exaggerated by the specialization of Roman society. While every adult male German was a seasonal soldier, each Roman legionary represented the defence effort of some tens or even hundreds of civilians. Though professional soldiery has advantages of discipline and experience and can usually be relied on to defeat several times their number of amateurs, their capacity for doing so is heavily dependent on their being well equipped, and it so happened that, at the moment when sheer numbers were beginning to tell against them, the legionaries found that their methods and equipment were hopelessly obsolete. The German soldier of the end of the fourth century had a better sword made of better steel, and the Goths had learnt the latest techniques of cavalry warfare from the nomads of the Russian steppe. The Romans were left dependent on discipline and generalship, and when these failed, as fail they must in the long run, on the hiring of Germans to fight Germans. This last could only be a stop-gap, for an indispensable soldier will set up on his own if even his most irresponsible demands are not met. In the end, the Western Empire was destroyed by the arms of the professional German soldiery that imperial necessity had created.

But if all this is true, why did not the East fall as well as the West? The answer here goes back to Julius Caesar, who, by conquering Gaul out of personal ambition, carried the Roman eagles into continental Europe. The Greeks and Carthaginians had colonized and economically unified the Mediterranean littoral, providing the basis for its political unification as achieved by Rome. Julius Caesar marched beyond the confines of this natural unit and introduced Mediterranean culture into France and England. There it flourished in an etiolated manner while the political climate was favourable. But when the Roman frontiers ceased to expand and defence costs began to rise, the slender trade of the north-west dried up in the hotter taxation, and the people left the cities, the foci of the tax man's attention. The West soon proved completely unable to pay its way. Once the division of the Empire became a reality and the West was deprived of the support of the far wealthier, far more urbanized East, it collapsed almost spontaneously. The East was just rich enough to buy off invaders and hire guards. Thus it survived ingloriously for a century and by Justinian's time had rebuilt a native army on new lines.

The relation of towns and trade to taxation potential is a vital one and the absence of sizeable towns and of organized trade routes in the West is a striking feature of Map 528E. The greater wealth of the townsman has less to do with his importance to the exchequer than his accessibility and his payment in cash, for the cost of collecting taxes in money is minimal. To gather a percentage of the produce of scattered, unco-operative peasantry, to transport it to where it can be marketed or utilized without exorbitant wastage, yields a very poor return. In the West, taxation killed the towns and trade and finally alienated the rural population. The house was ready to fall when someone knocked at the door.

FEUDAL SOCIETY

To escape the rapacity of the Roman tax collector, peasants in the later days of the Roman Empire often put themselves under the protection of the biggest of the local landowners. In return for the title to the peasant's land, the landowner guarded the civil interests of his client and as far as possible shielded him from taxes. This seems a hard bargain from the peasant's point of view, for he surrendered his freehold and became a tenant whom the landlord could evict at will; and it is a telling measure of the burden of taxation that in the last century of the Western Empire the freeholding peasantry voluntarily liquidated itself. The landlord gained all round. He tended to take his increasing rent in produce where possible, for the less money there was about, the less the taxgatherer took. It became necessary for him to live on his land and not in a distant town, and he soon came to administer the everyday life of his estate and its practically rightless peasantry as though the central authority did not exist.

The Germans who overran the West were fighting men, owing allegiance to the head of their band which they had expressed in an oath at the beginning of the campaign. In an era of continuous warfare, it might have been given to the same man for many years and there was a growing tendency for the successful leader of a tribal group of war-bands to become accepted as a permanent King. Previously, the Kingship had been a temporary post, created only to answer a sudden emergency, and even when it became life-long it was not at first a prerogative of any one house. The rules of succession evolved slowly as an inflexible system proved the simplest method of avoiding a sanguinary contest at the coronation. By then, the Germans were largely settled on Roman land and the members of war-band had become landowners. They still owed an obligation of military service in time of trouble to the chief of the old war-band and he to the King. The peasants passively accepted the arbitrary rule of the new landowner and paid him rent in kind or in labour in return for his protection. They probably found him cheaper to support than a Roman

whose standard of living was related to city life; his protection extended into the military sphere where the Roman had been impotent.

The society formed by this fusion of late Roman and German systems is called feudal. It is essentially a replacement of law and money by obligation and tithe. The original Roman ideal of government and the feudal one can be schematically compared thus:

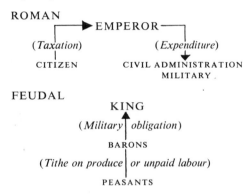

The difference between the two is, however, greater than this, for whereas the government was only a part of the Roman's life, feudalism permeated a medieval man's existence. The Romans distinguished, as we do now, between freeholder and tenant. To a Frenchman of the eleventh century, everyone, baron or peasant, held his fief[1] as a tenant, for to keep it he had to render dues of some sort (produce, labour, military service) to his overlord. Yet on the other hand, while he rendered his dues, he could not be evicted from his fief and he could pass it on to his heirs, so that in some ways he held it outright. There was thus a complete fusion of economic and political obligation in the reciprocal relationship of fief-giver and holder, lord and vassal.

'Barons' in the feudal diagram requires subdivision, for the oath taken by the smallest barons (knights) referred to their local leader, his to a provincial superior, and only the biggest barons owed allegiance direct to the King. Also the military obligation was purely defensive, and if a King wished to wage offensive war he had to attract followers by a promise of plunder or position. At home, quarrels between barons were continuous and often settled by force, though there was a tendency to request the arbitration of the King. A powerful personality at the top could make the whole system seem more closely knit than it was, but a King's actual power depended on the size of the royal domain – the land owned directly by him or by his own knights.

It will be seen that the great thing about feudalism was its cheapness. Though the justice administered within its framework was of a very inferior sort it did protect the peasant at minimal cost. Ultimately, the peasant depended on the good nature of his baron, and one has to have considerable faith in mankind to hope for a disinterested decision when, for example, a rent tribunal is composed entirely of landlords. But the later history of the Roman Empire had proved that justice can cost more than it is worth, and the feudal system came as a relief to a povertystricken Europe. By Carolingian times, it had begun to be formalized[2] and was working fairly well.

1. Usually land, but not always. A court or military appointment could equally be a fief, and once you start to think in this weird way it is difficult to draw the line anywhere.

2. The earlier German Kingdoms in Western Europe still possessed a considerable amount of the Roman machinery of government and for a long time Kings' representatives (counts) were appointed for each administrative district. As the appointment soon became hereditary and the local barons could obtain from the King an 'immunity' which guaranteed their independence, count became merely another feudal title.

However, from its particulate nature, feudalism was unsuitable for large Empires and the final Carolingian flowering was bound to wither. In fact, in this the feudal system was self-correcting, for if there were two or more sons the King's inheritance was always divided between them.

For reasons of economy, the Byzantines too toyed with feudal institutions. They set up peasant communities on state land which returned military service instead of rent. On occasion they even swallowed their feeling that it was dangerous to give the civil and military administration of an area to a single man and split the Empire into baronial-type units. But the magnates were always subject to a strict state control, and in the end the Empire always reverted to a tax-paying peasantry and a professional army.

The feudal system began to decline when, around 1000, Europe became sufficiently wealthy to afford a limited return to centralized government. The two Norman Kingdoms led the way, the Norman genius being assisted by the previous history of the lands they conquered. In England, the Roman element had been nearly exterminated in the slow Anglo–Saxon advance and the land re-peopled by immigrants from Germany. The result was a society akin to the primitive German, and though later influences from the continent caused a superficial feudalization there was never the same outlook as there was in France. The Normans who won England, being few, could only hope to hold their prize if they observed a military discipline and, although he utilized feudal forms, William in fact organized the new state in a manner that made him the effective authority throughout the land. Southern Italy had been recently Byzantine when seized by Guiscard and it was easy for him to revive the machinery of autocracy, though again the terminology was largely feudal. The small size of these kingdoms suited them for

the role they played in re-introducing centralization. They did not strain the simple communications of the times, and they showed that, on such a scale at least, the new method of government was economical and efficient. As the national income in the West continued to rise and money returned to a dominant place in everyday life, the deficiencies of feudalism became more obvious. It became harder to bear with the local eccentricities that were its inevitable adjunct, to circumvent its inflexibility, and to counter its basic lawlessness. The merchants and the peasants found their champion in the King, who, by hair-splitting insistence on his feudal rights and by revival of decayed precedent, often managed to wear down the unsubordinate baronage or to drive them to a revolt in which they could be destroyed. Royal propaganda encouraged the growth of national as opposed to provincial patriotism; it appealed to the memory of Roman greatness and Roman law. To the end of the Middle Ages, however, the size of the area in which such a process could be more than temporarily successful remained limited. France corresponded to the maximum. The German Empire was well above it and ultimately the centrifugal forces split it into a maze of big and little fiefs whose histories of devouring and dividing are like the circular stories of pond life.

Merchant and monarch were both concerned to limit the power of the baronage and, as this task required their active alliance, the basic fissure between the interests of the two rarely showed during the Middle Ages. When the feudal system produced a complete fragmentation of authority, and where the towns were large and rich, the richest and most powerful merchants could set up an oligarchical government of their own. The republics of Novgorod and Venice are examples of the type of urban plutocracy that resulted, and

there were others in Germany, Italy, and north Russia. Even in the bloom of their prosperity, such city states were always liable to capture by an indigenous or foreign despot, and of them all only Venice, the wealthiest and the best defended by nature, managed to preserve her freedom.

The oligarchy was as far along the road towards democracy as medieval man ever saw. In most countries, the vast mass of the population was peasantry, sullen and asking only to be left alone. Extreme wretchedness occasioned a few hopeless risings (France 1357, Germany 1450) of blind bestial fury; in England, the only disturbance was a riot for better wages (1381) which was as politically dumb as these. Similarly, the only explosions of the urban proletariat came in times of depression and, though in this case revolts in Flanders (1328) and Florence (1379) did lead to the temporary erection of 'popular' governments, these failed because the miseries they were supposed to alleviate were caused by economic factors rather than misrule. There was never any spontaneous emotion in favour of democracy in the Middle Ages and it was only in the sickness of the state that such aberrations were seen.

THE NOMADS

Although nomadism is a more primitive state than agriculturalism it is scarcely less specialized, and in the medieval period nomad societies often possessed a culture comparable in level of attainment to that in the contemporary settled communities. Flocks of sheep, goats, and horses provide all the raw materials necessary for a simple life and a good many luxuries too. Indeed, in wealth the nomad often exceeded the agriculturalist, for, if his pasture was poor in quality, it was nearly limitless in extent, and while he could keep moving his herds could be of great size.

The ability to move far and fast was the keynote of the nomad's existence and the root of his success in war. Napoleon's dictum of military 'momentum' states that the real strength of an army is the product of its size and speed. Nomad armies, in which every man was not only horsed but had a spare mount in tow, could move at a speed that for the era was phenomenal. Because of this mobility they gave a totally misleading impression of enormous numbers, and the word horde, originally a term for a Turko-Mongol regiment, came to mean an innumerable swarm. This erroneous impression was strengthened by the nomads' locust-like capacity for thorough destruction which stemmed partly from the harshness of steppe and desert life, partly from their compelling hate and fear of the ever-multiplying peasants. Terror spread before a nomad advance and did much to prepare the way for victory.

There is another analogy with locusts which is worth pursuing: locusts usually live out their lives as solitary grasshoppers in the areas of scrub which are scattered through the desert. A succession of good years causes an enlargement of the scrub islands and consequently of the locust population; if the next year is catastrophically bad, the islands shrink to a fraction of their original size and the locusts are crowded together. The sight of hundreds of others of his kind, milling about in front of him, stimulates the individual locust to metamorphose. When the change to the migratory form is complete, the whole swarm rises in a cloud from the island they have eaten bare and sets out for pastures new.

How big a part such purely climatic causes played in initiating nomadic movements is debatable. Attempts have been made to relate the history of Asiatic movement to a cyclical desiccation of the continent, but probably the mechanism of explosive migration is much too sensitive to be a guide to long-term fluctuations. It is obvious, however, that physical factors of this type were responsible for much of the unrest that at times took hold of the nomadic world and which is usually described in purely political terms.

Of the four great nomadic nations, the Arabs, Berbers, Turks, and Mongols, the first two have histories which are part of the greater story of Islam. Their successes led them to give up nomadism and settle on the lands they had conquered and though occasionally new tribes (Murabits, Qarmatians) swept from the desert to overthrow the Empires established by their forebears, there was never any attempt to impose the desert way of life on the settled communities of the Near-East area. The Turks and Mongols were far more intolerant and nearly always ignored the habits of the populations they made themselves masters of. They regarded irrigation works and other means of increasing the fertility of the land as impediments to grazing and only desired to turn the soil back to pasture. They had a simple answer to the problem of surplus population which such a drop in productivity entailed.

The military prowess of the Turko-Mongols and the habitually ruthless way in which it was exploited brought considerable gains to the nomadic world. The Huns, Avars, and Magyars in turn brought the Hungarian steppe within the Asiatic orbit, the Seljuks did the same for Anatolia, while the borders of the steppe were nearly always under nomad domination and the writ of the great Khans extended far beyond. Yet at the end of the Middle Ages, the struggle was going against the nomad simply because pastoralism can support only a small population. As is most evident in the struggle between China and the nomads on her northern border, it was the reproductive superiority of the agriculturalist that won the day. The expanding mass of Chinese continually overflowed the wall that had been built to keep the Tartar out, and no massacre could more than momentarily stop the numerical aggression of the peasantry. The nomad might appear in hordes before the eyes of the terrified; to the nomad, the constant multiplication of his enemies was a sober fact that in the end must squeeze him out of existence. When the townsmen's technology ended the military superiority of the nomad, the battle had already been won. Hungary had been incorporated into Christendom and the Turks of Anatolia were tilling the fields they had desolated. Ottomans and Timurids, the last Turkish conquerors, built their armies around an infantry core.

*

This book does not pretend to be one of original scholarship or research; it is a compilation. In the often tedious work involved in bringing it to press I have been much assisted by the encouragement of my brother Brian McEvedy, by the informed and erudite comment of Peter Fison, by the secretarial efficiency of Kate McKinnon Wood, and by the general and essential aid furnished by my wife.

A NOTE ON MOUNTAINS AND TERRAIN

Rivers, the only physical features shown in the base map of this book, are often chosen by man as his boundaries, but mountain barriers impose themselves on political geography and consequently deserve at least equal attention. Unfortunately they are impossible to display unobtrusively and have had to be relegated to this map in company with an equally necessary indication of the general character of the terrain.

The simplest and most convincing examples of mountain frontiers are the Pyrenees and Alps, which partially seal off the Iberian and Italian peninsulas. Minor ranges isolate Bohemia; the Carpathians give Hungary a natural border in the east; the Byzantines were able to recuperate from the defeats of the eighth century by sheltering behind the Taurus. Some ranges of equal height were of less importance. The Atlas merely parallels the edge of the Sahara; the Iranian plateau rarely appears in political isolation because its master characteristically dominated neighbouring entities such as Mesopotamia; though Epirus occasionally escaped the rule of Constantinople thanks to the mountains between them, frontiers within the Balkans are more often the result of conflict between a sea power and a land power (Byzantines versus Slavs and Bulgars; Venetians versus Byzantines and Ottomans) than the outlines of natural territorial units; similarly the Apennines never perturbed the habitually transverse division of Italy. But a look through the book will enable the reader to make his own deductions.

In early medieval times, the contrast between Europe, with the major part of its land potentially arable, and the lands of the south Mediterranean littoral and Near East, with only occasional strips of good land, was less striking than it might seem. The area actually under cultivation in the West was only a fraction of the possible, the rest being forest, and at any one time half the cleared land was lying fallow. In Egypt and Mesopotamia the rivers brought not only water but fertilizing silt, and in the strong sun the yields were enormously higher[1] and populations correspondingly denser. After 1000, forest clearance in Europe tipped the balance towards Christendom (previous to that date it probably only equalled the abandonment of exhausted land); whereas the population of the near East at the end of the medieval period was probably less and certainly no more than it had been in Roman times, the western provinces showed an increase of the order of 50–100 per cent and Eastern Europe, one may guess, an even greater rise. The conifer forests of northern latitudes remained, of course, entirely virgin and insignificantly inhabited.

1. In Mesopotamia over-irrigation had its dangers as it could in time raise the water table, which is saline, to a level at which crops were affected. It has been suggested that this, rather than Hulagu's visitation, was the cause of Mesopotamia's decline in the late medieval period.

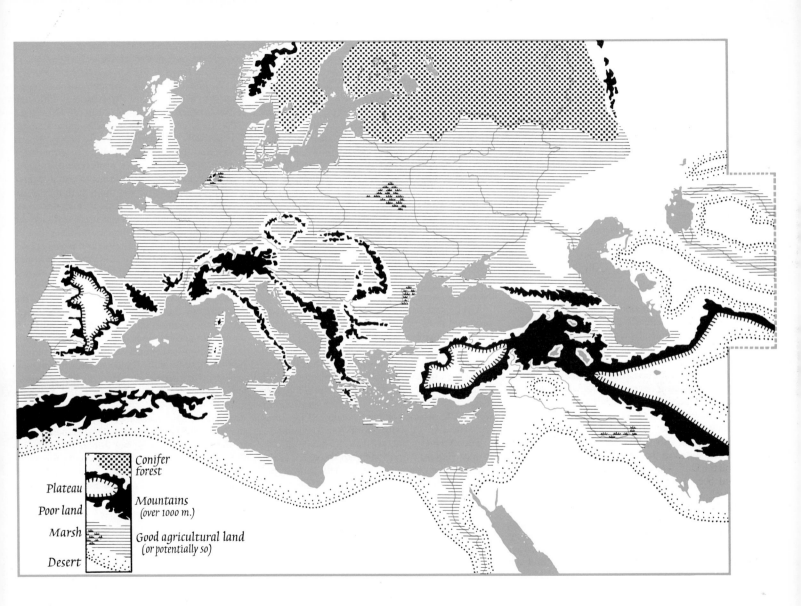

Conifer forest

Plateau

Poor land

Marsh

Desert

Mountains (over 1000 m.)

Good agricultural land (or potentially so)

362

Augustus, the first Roman Emperor (27 B.C. – A.D. 14), either considering that the Empire had reached its natural limits or embittered by his own failure to subdue Germany, advised his successors against further expansion, and this advice was, by and large, followed. The conquest of Germany would have eliminated a dangerous enemy and shortened the Roman line, but it was never attempted again, though in the century following the death of Augustus the Romans had a clear military superiority. The few extra provinces which were acquired in this period were of little value and with one exception had been lost again by the date of the first map in this series. The exception was Britain, whose conquest, begun by Claudius (41–54), was probably necessary to protect the coast of France. (It also meant that the Romans had practically completed their conquest of the Celts. Of Spain, North Italy, France, and the British Isles, only Ireland and Pictish Scotland remained free.) The Empire was on the defensive after the death of Trajan (98–117), but for a long while it maintained its territory and, repulsed in their many attempts to break through the Rhine–Danube frontier, the teeming Germans turned east for the needed *Lebensraum*. Prominent in this movement were the Goths, who in the third century reached the Black Sea where they established two confederacies, that of the Visigoths (West Goths) and that of the Ostrogoths (East Goths). The Ostrogoths adopted a nomadic way of life, suited to the steppe, between the Dnieper and the Don, which was the centre of their power, and became masters of a vast tract of country which reached back to their original Baltic homelands. Then as now the Slavs formed the basic population of Eastern Europe and European Russia; only the few who fled northwards among the Finnish peoples and preserved their freedom are visible in this map. As the Ostrogoths at the

peak of their power, under the near-legendary king Ermanarich, advanced beyond the Don, they came into contact with the Alans, an Iranian people nomadizing in the Caucasus, and with the Huns, who were the vanguard of the Asiatics.

The Goths were the strongest of the Germans and the most adventurous; in Germany itself there was no nation of comparable power. The tribes were antagonistic to each other and disunited within themselves. Only in times of crisis did a tribe elect a king; it was the political and organizational superiority of the Romans which was the most important factor in the preservation of the Empire in later centuries. The Frankish and Alemannian confederations were the most troublesome; the tribes not actually on the frontier were little known, although the Angles and Saxons raided the coasts of Britain and France. The Frisians, however, who were the main power in the North Sea, were friendly to the Romans.

The Eastern frontier of the Roman Empire was protected in its northern part by the buffer states of Lazica,[1] Iberia, and Armenia, but in Mesopotamia the Roman and Persian Empires were in direct contact. Persia, traditionally hostile, was the only state that rivalled Rome in stability and civilization; between the two there were frequent if typically indecisive wars. East of the Persians were the Kushans, holding the valley of the Oxus and extending into both central Asia and India.

The Arabian and African frontiers of the Roman Empire correspond with the edges of the Arabian and African deserts. The Arabs and Berbers who inhabited these inhospitable places were a nuisance to the Empire but never more than a local danger.

If the frontiers of the Roman Empire had changed little in three and a half centuries, the Empire itself was very different from that of Augustus. The requirements of the military,

always burdensome, had become crushing as the population and power of Rome's enemies had increased. Towards the end of the third century, the Empire had nearly disintegrated under the attacks of Germans and Persians, and, although it was saved, the reorganization by Diocletian (284–305) created what was really a new Empire. Theoretically at least, the whole economy was frozen and then taxed to the limit to provide for the increasingly expensive professional soldiery. Defence became the prime concern and in consequence a good general was the best Emperor. As a corollary of this, the separate frontiers required separate commands, and it was usual to divide the Empire into western and eastern halves in line with the division between Latin and Greek speaking populations. The victory of Christianity, which further transformed the Empire, is dealt with in a separate section.

In contradiction to these various trends, the year 362 saw the Empire united and officially reverting to paganism under the Emperor Julian. A competent general, he had decisively defeated the last Franco–Alemannic invasion of France, though he allowed some of the Franks to settle in Belgium, retaining their tribal organization while acknowledging the supremacy of Rome (358). This formula (the term '*foederatii*' was later used to describe such tribes) had already been applied to the North British and was to be used increasingly in the next fifty years; but Julian probably regarded it as a temporary expedient, necessary because first internal dissensions and then Persian attacks required his presence and army in the East.

1. Lazica and Iberia were the twin Kingdoms of the Georgians, and had been virtually christianized. The more primitive Abasgians, also of Georgian stock, remained heathen.

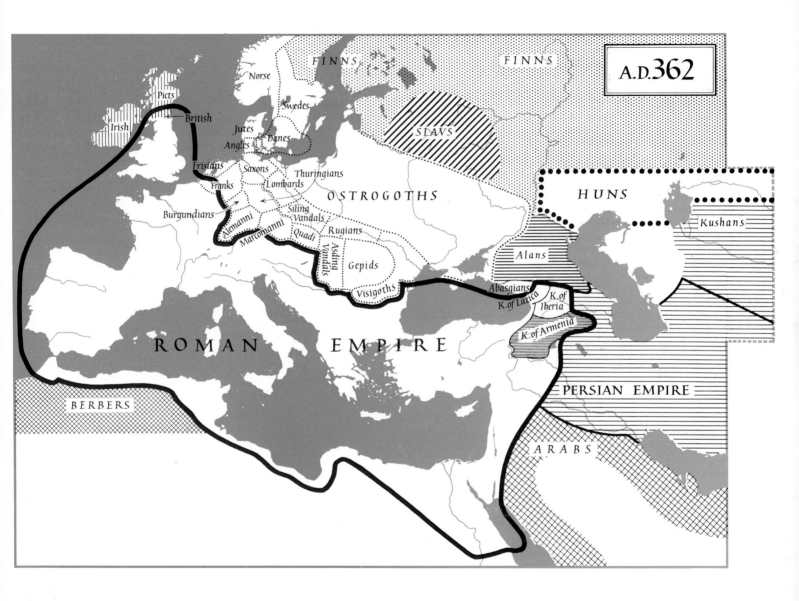

406

Julian's expedition against Persia ended in disaster. He himself was killed and the army only extricated after his successor had signed a treaty by which the Empire ceded the Eastern half of Roman Mesopotamia, while Iberia and Armenia became Persian vassals (364). By and large the Romans kept these terms, though they found it difficult to resist interfering in Armenia. In the end the kingdom was divided between the two with the Persians getting four-fifths of the country (387). The Romans accepted this bad bargain with relief, for it was by this time essential to have peace on the eastern frontier. Their misfortunes there were only a moon-cast shadow of what was taking place in Europe.

In 372, the steady eastward expansion of the Ostrogoths provoked an explosive reaction from the Huns of the Volga steppe. Ermanarich saw his armies swallowed up by the nomad hordes and his great empire crumble away. The Huns rolled forward to the Danube, crushing the Visigoths and enslaving the Gepids, who had the misfortune to occupy the Hungarian steppe (375). There they settled down with their flocks, lords of a pasture that stretched back to the Caspian. In three years they had obliterated a century of German expansion.

While the Gepids remained where they were as vassals of the Huns, the Goths and Asding Vandals applied to the Roman Empire for sanctuary. The Romans allotted them lands along the Danube frontier, but acted so overbearingly that by 378 the Visigoths had broken out in revolt against their new masters. The army that the Eastern Emperor led to quell the revolt was annihilated by the Gothic cavalry at Adrianople. Cavalry had demonstrated that it was the decisive arm and the legions were never resurrected; as the Romans had little cavalry, their army was from now on largely composed of German or Hunnish mercenaries, and it was not long before barbarian generals were wielding considerable political power in consequence of this dependence. The Visigoths, unable to take fortified towns, could not pluck the fruits of their victory and were temporarily pacified by a mixture of diplomacy and blockade (382). They broke out again in 396 to be similarly re-settled, this time in Epirus (north-west Greece), a position from which they could advance on either half of the Empire. In 402–3 they invaded Italy only to be beaten back by the skill of Stilicho the Vandal, who commanded the army of the West. While they recovered in Yugoslavia, Stilicho was able to defeat a formidable coalition of Ostrogoths, Quadi, and Asding Vandals (405), but to defend Italy he was forced to strip the Rhine frontier of troops. The next year, a coalition of Marcomanni, Quadi,[1] and Asding and Siling Vandals, together with a clan of Alans who had fled from the Hun-dominated Caucasus, moved westward towards the now defenceless province of France. On the last day of 406 they crossed the frozen Rhine at Mainz.

1. The German tribes along the upper Danube, the Ale-manni, Marcomanni, and Quadi, were known collectively as Suevi. In following the fortunes of the coalition of 406 in subsequent maps, the term is used to denote the Marcomanno–Quadic contingent.

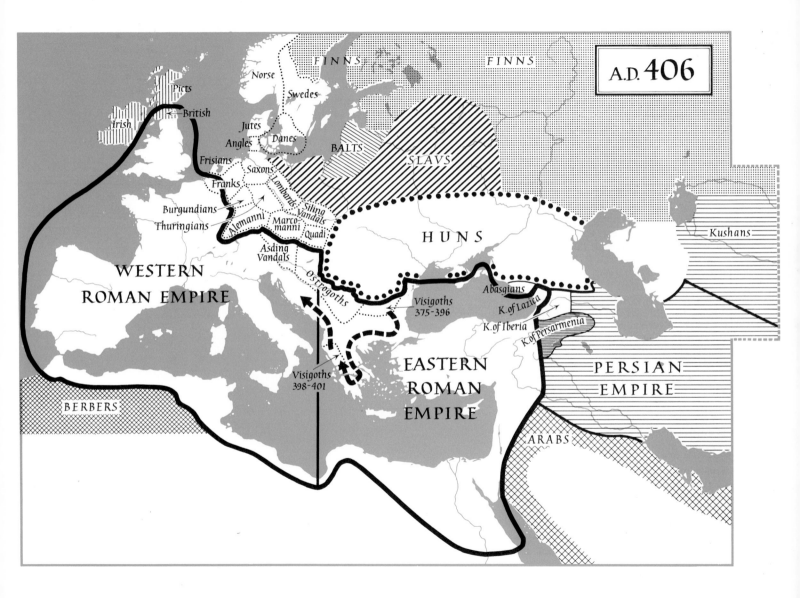

A.D. 406

FINNS   FINNS

Norse

Swedes

Picts

British

Irish

Jutes

Angles   Danes

Frisians

Saxons

Franks

Lombards

Burgundians

Thuringians

Alemanni

Marco-manni

Silina Vandals

Quadi

Asding Vandals

Ostrogoths

WESTERN ROMAN EMPIRE

BALTS

SLAVS

HUNS

Visigoths 375-396

Abasgians

K. of Lazica

K. of Iberia

K. of Persarmenia

Kushans

Visigoths 398-401

EASTERN ROMAN EMPIRE

PERSIAN EMPIRE

BERBERS

ARABS

420

There was nothing to oppose the ravages of the Alan–Vandal–Suevic horde which swarmed over France in 407; the only possibility of deliverance lay in the garrison of Britain, which had revolted and set up a soldier Emperor of its own. He did indeed cross the Channel in force, and ostensibly it was to pacify the province, which the authorities at Rome appeared to have abandoned, but in fact he simply sought support for his usurped imperial title from the Franks, Burgundians, and Alemanni, who had taken advantage of the collapse of the frontier to annex the left bank of the Rhine. The Alans, Vandals, and Suevi were allowed to cross the Pyrenees and seize lands along the Atlantic seaboard of Spain (409). The only other effect of his revolt was that, in taking with him the troops from Britain, he left the country with no defence against the Anglo–Saxon raids, except for what the unwillingly independent provincials could provide from their own resources. In the end he was easily captured and executed by a Roman army that would have been better employed elsewhere (411), while England slipped out of the Roman orbit into Celtic anarchy.

When in 408 Stilicho was murdered by the Emperor, who distrusted his ambition, the Italian core of the Empire, for which so much had been sacrificed, was immediately forfeit. The Empire had existed for so long that no one could imagine an alternative; the barbarians asked only for land and subsidies in lieu of plunder, their leaders for military commands within the framework of the imperial system. Once Stilicho was dead, Alaric King of the Visigoths presented his demands at the gates of Rome and, though at first he was conciliatory, the refusal of the Western authorities (safe in the new and impregnable capital of Ravenna) to meet his claims led to the storming of the city (410). Although the actual sack was mild and almost respectful, the prestige of the Roman world fell with the ancient centre of its greatness, and now that its helplessness was blazoned abroad the ransoms asked by its enemies grew. Yet Alaric's successors were still sufficiently impressed by the civilization they held at their mercy to work to preserve it. In the Imperial service the Visigoths entered Gaul (412), where another rival emperor who had been created by the Franks and Alemanni was disposed of (413). They then moved to Spain (414), attacking the states founded by the Alan–Vandal–Suevic invaders. The Siling Vandals and Alans were exterminated (416); the Suevi and Asding Vandals only saved by the Romans who, fearful of the Visigoths becoming all powerful, prematurely persuaded them to retire to the extensive lands in south-west France which were the reward of their labours. The new Visigothic Kingdom was free from even nominal imperial suzerainty; there was now no formula to disguise the break-up of Roman power.

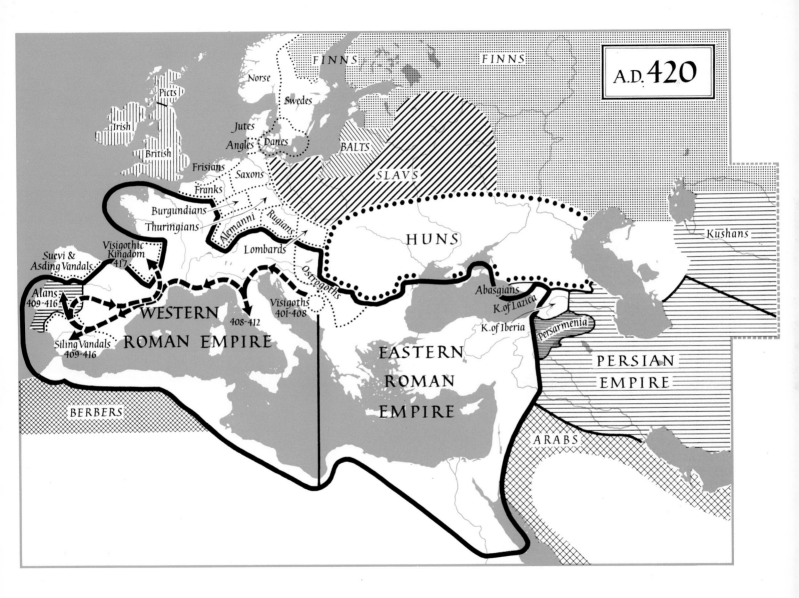

A.D. 420

FINNS   FINNS

Norse

Swedes

Picts

Irish

Jutes

British

Angles Danes

BALTS

SLAVS

Frisians

Saxons

Franks

Burgundians

Alemanni   Rugians

HUNS

Thuringians

Lombards

Kushans

Visigothic
Kingdom
417

Suevi &
Asding Vandals

Ostrogoths

Abasgians

Alans
409-416

WESTERN

408-412

Visigoths
401-408

K. of Lazica

K. of Iberia

Persarmenia

Siling Vandals
409-416

ROMAN EMPIRE

EASTERN

ROMAN

PERSIAN

EMPIRE

EMPIRE

BERBERS

ARABS

450

For a generation after their rush to the Danube, the Huns were remarkably quiet, but under Attila (433–53) they made full use of their strength and of the weakness of both halves of the Empire. They extracted lands and enormous subsidies from the Eastern Empire, and extended their dominion over Germany, decimating the Burgundians (436), who were resettled as foederates by the Romans round Geneva (443). Only the (Salian) Franks in north-east France escaped their rule; the Alemanni, the (Ripuarian) Franks of the Rhine, and all the tribes to their east were vassals of the Hun.

In 451 Attila led his army and its German auxiliaries into France. A motley body of Romans, Burgundians, and Salian Franks, with a Visigothic backbone, gathered to oppose him. Attila fell back from Orleans (the westernmost point reached by any of the Altaian conquerors) and the armies met at the Campus Mauriacus. The battle was hard-fought but inconclusive – the first check Attila had received – but though he withdrew to Hungary his power was little impaired. Next year he raided Italy in strength and had to be bought off. That winter he died, and the Empire he passed on to his too-numerous sons was destroyed by a German revolt. Led by the Gepids, the Germans crushed their overlords at the battle of the Nedao (454).

While Europe was paralysed and almost united by the menace of Attila, Africa was invaded by the Asding Vandals (428), who blackmailed the best provinces from the Romans, anxious to preserve the African corn supply for Italy (442). Their King Gaiseric, wily and ruthless, consolidated his power and built himself a fleet.

England, forgotten by Rome, was raided by almost everyone else – Picts, Irish, Angles, Saxons, Jutes, and Frisians. The Jutes[1] even began a permanent settlement in the south-east (449). Some of the Britons escaped from all this by crossing to France, where they founded an independent community in the Brest peninsula and became known as Bretons.

The power of the Kushans, the Eastern neighbours of the Persians, had been declining steadily from its peak in the second century A.D. By the beginning of the fifth century the Kushans had become thoroughly Persianized: and when they were swept away by the white Huns (440), a Mongolian Tribe which migrated from the Altai region at this time, Persia lost a shield rather than an enemy. The newcomers proved extremely aggressive, terrorizing both the eastern provinces of the Persian Empire and the remnant of the Kushans in Afghanistan.

1. This is the classical view, but it seems likely that Jutland in Denmark was overrun by the Danes a considerable time before the conquest of south-east England, and that this was the work of Frisian tribes. These may have included Jutes displaced from Denmark and temporarily settled in Frisia.

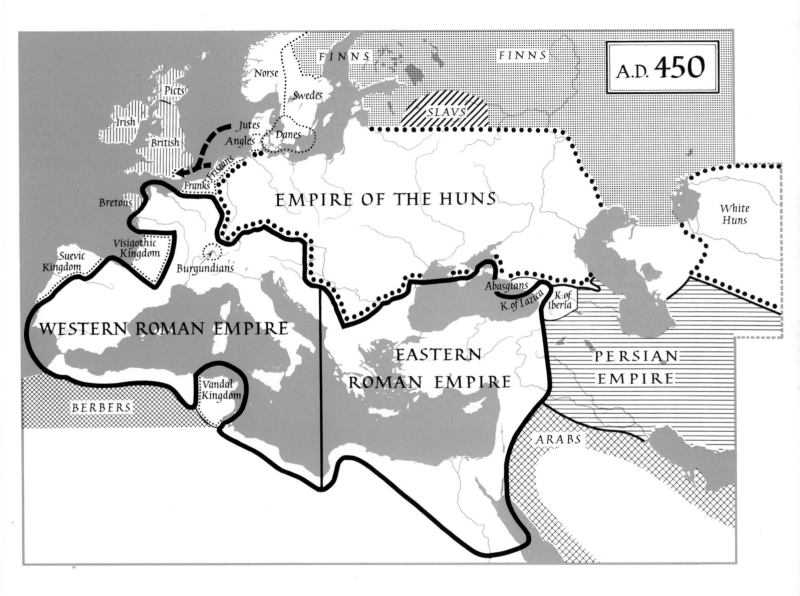

FINNS   FINNS

Norse

Swedes

SLAVS

Picts

Irish

British

Jutes
Angles   Danes

Frisians

Franks

EMPIRE OF THE HUNS

A.D. 450

White
Huns

Bretons

Visigothic
Kingdom

Burgundians

Suevic
Kingdom

WESTERN ROMAN EMPIRE

Abasgians
K. of Lazica   K. of
Iberia

EASTERN
ROMAN EMPIRE

PERSIAN
EMPIRE

Vandal
Kingdom

BERBERS

ARABS

476

After the disaster at the Nedao, some of the Huns remained for a few years in Hungary, raiding the Eastern Empire. When they found that even this was beyond their strength, they followed their brethren who had returned to the Russian steppe (470). On the shores of the Sea of Azov, the two contingents, known as Kutrigurs and Utigurs, bickered over the sorry remnant of the Empire of Attila. Next to them, in the Crimea, a pocket of Ostrogoths survived as a memento of Ermanarich's likewise vanished glory.

The full extent of the Slavs is now revealed. Hidden before by the Ostrogothic and Hunnish Empires, the Slavs had occupied the lands east of the Oder, and north and east of the Carpathians, stretching to the upper Don in Russia. Now they moved into the territories the Germans had left vacant, and their western and southern boundaries became the Elbe and the lower Danube. Of the main groups of Slavs, the Antes of south Russia were the wealthiest and most powerful, but politically all the Slavs, as well as the related Balts, were very backward. Their myriad chieftains lacked all sense of unity and were therefore easily dominated by other races.

The final stage in the disintegration of the Western Empire has now been reached. The Visigoths expanded to the Loire and the Rhône (470) in France and conquered Spain (469–78) except for the parts occupied by the previous Suevic invaders and by the aboriginal and almost inaccessible Basques. The Burgundians established a considerable domain, stretching from Switzerland to the Mediterranean, while the Franks and the Alemanni advanced more gradually. Italy was in the hands of Odoacer, a barbarian general who finally dispensed with puppet emperors (476), and acknowledging instead the suzerainty of the Eastern Emperor, with the proviso that no attempt be made to realize it, reigned as King of Italy. Of the Western Empire there remained only Dalmatia, where dwelt until 480 an Emperor officially recognized by the East; the north-west quarter of France was still in Roman hands, but as the independent Kingdom of Soissons, the creation of a revolted general, not as part of the Empire.

Before the Western Empire lost the last of its land, it had lost its command of the sea. The foresight of the Vandal King Gaiseric in building a fleet now enabled him to dominate the Mediterranean. After completing the conquest of Africa (455), he annexed the Balearics, Corsica, Sardinia, and the western end of Sicily, while his raiders brought back the plunder of both West and East. The Vandal sack of Rome in 455 was far more thorough and business-like than Alaric's. But apart from Vandal raids, the Eastern Empire[1] was given a breathing space in which to repair and renew itself.

1. Officially the extinction of the Western half restored the unity of the Empire, but it is useful to retain the geographical qualification as a measure of the many differences between the classical Empire of Rome and the Roman Empire of Constantinople.

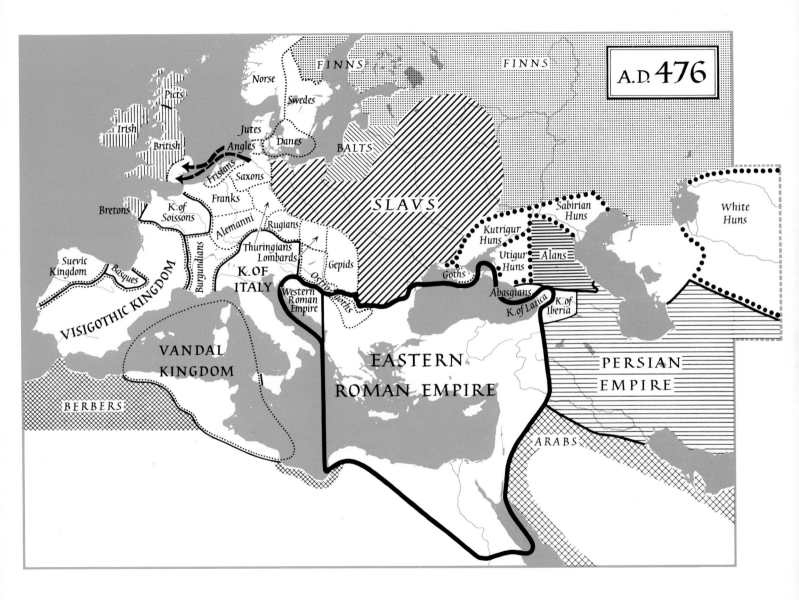

A.D. 476

FINNS · FINNS

Norse · Swedes
Picts
Irish
British · Jutes · Danes
Angles · BALTS
Frisians · SLAVS
Saxons
Bretons · Franks
K. of · Alemanni · Rugians
Soissons
Suevic · Thuringians · Gepids
Kingdom · Basques · Lombards
VISIGOTHIC KINGDOM · Burgundians · K. OF · Ostrogoths
ITALY · Western
Roman
Empire · Goths

Sabirian Huns
Kutrigur Huns
Utigur Huns · Alans · White Huns
Abasgians
K. of Lazica
K. of Iberia

VANDAL
KINGDOM · EASTERN
ROMAN EMPIRE · PERSIAN
EMPIRE

BERBERS

ARABS

528

The final fall of the Western Empire did not bring stability to the German states that had grown up in its place. Odoacer, who had pretensions to the Imperial inheritance, annexed Dalmatia on the death of its 'Emperor' (480); and when the Rugians crossed the Danube from Bohemia he defeated them so crushingly that they vanish from history (487); their place in Bohemia was taken by a confederacy of Suevic remnants, the Bavarians. Odoacer's success stimulated the mistrust of the Eastern Romans. The government of Constantinople had been having increasing trouble with its Ostrogothic foederates, and, as it stood to profit by his success or failure, encouraged Theodoric the Ostrogoth to invade Italy. After a hard-fought war (489–93) and some judicious treachery, Theodoric made himself master of an enlarged Italian Kingdom. The new Gothic power was established just in time to prevent the complete collapse of the old.

By assassinating some of his rivals and executing the remainder for complicity, Clovis made himself sole King of the Franks. In 486 he annexed the Kingdom of Soissons and in 505 the lands of the Alemanni, except for a portion which Theodoric took under his protection and incorporated in the Ostrogothic Kingdom. But Clovis's most important achievement was his victory over the Visigoths at Vouillé (507), after which he would have run them out of France altogether if Theodoric had not intervened again. Theodoric took the Provençal coast from the Burgundians (they had lost it to the Visigoths in 481 and had only just regained it after the Visigothic *débâcle*). He then defeated the Franks and retained for the Visigoths the strip of Mediterranean France known as Septimania. The death of Clovis (511) and the division of his Kingdom between his four sons[1] weakened the Franks, and their dismal attempt to annex Burgundy profited only Theodoric, who increased his

holding in Provence. As Theodoric also ruled the Visigothic realm on behalf of its boy-king, the prestige of the Goths was never higher. It was even sufficient to make the Vandals give up their toehold in Sicily without argument.

The Persians had been unable to take advantage of the embarrassments of the Roman Empire as they had had nomad trouble of their own. In attempting to defend the eastern provinces from the annual inroads of the White Huns, the Persian King finally lost his life and army (484). The Empire was left at the mercy of the victors, who, however, in true nomad fashion, contented themselves with a measure of control and an immoderate tribute. Their attentions were increasingly directed to India, the gateway to which had been in their hands since their elimination of the Kushans of Afghanistan (*c.* 460). Persia breathed again, but softly.

1. The partition was not simple, for each son held estates in each part of the country. The resulting 'kingdoms' are therefore not easily shown on a map of this scale, and indeed to show them would be to attach a false significance to them, as the Frankish Kingdom was regarded as a single unit governed jointly by four kings.

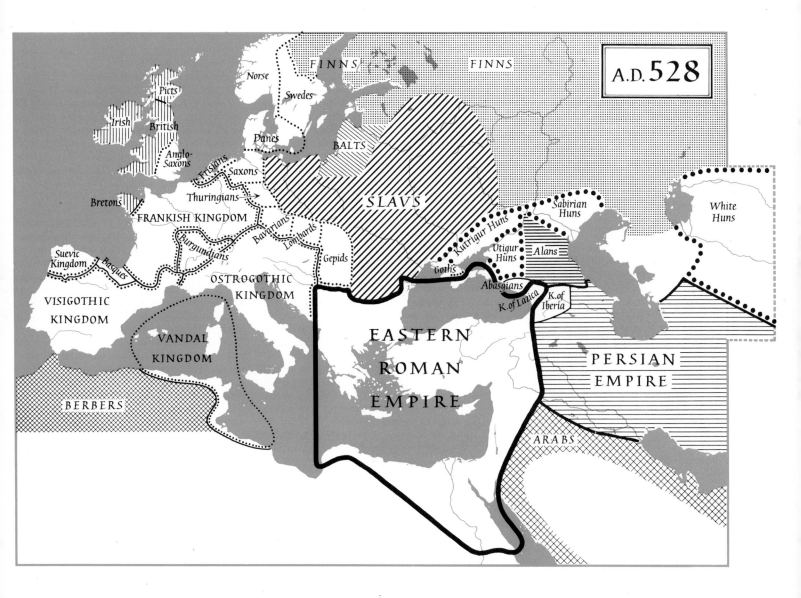

A.D. 528

FINNS   FINNS

Norse

Swedes

Picts

Irish   British

Danes

BALTS

Anglo-Saxons

Frisians

Saxons

Bretons

Thuringians

FRANKISH KINGDOM

Bavarians

Burgundians

Lombards

SLAVS

Gepids

Suevic Kingdom

Basques

OSTROGOTHIC KINGDOM

Goths

Kutrigur Huns

Sabirian Huns

White Huns

Utigur Huns

Alans

VISIGOTHIC KINGDOM

Abasgians

K. of Lazica

K. of Iberia

VANDAL KINGDOM

PERSIAN EMPIRE

BERBERS

EASTERN ROMAN EMPIRE

ARABS

The fourth century saw the triumph of the Christian Church. At its start, Christians were still persecuted; by the end, the adoption of any other religion by an Emperor was unthinkable, and the Church was unassailable. This victory of Christianity over paganism was a walkover, for its dogma was simpler, its ethical and social message more progressive, and its organization, rivalling that of the state, both efficient and militant. With in addition a clear superiority in prodigy and miracle, the only surprise is that the martyrs should have been so many. Perhaps this was due to the demand for relics – the machinery used in many executions seems to have been designed with the intention of producing varied remains.

Armenia became the first Christian state (303); the Roman Empire followed (337), and though the Emperor Julian disestablished and disavowed Christianity he failed to revivify the ancient beliefs. His synthetic neo-Platonism, which borrowed the structure and outbid the superstition of its rival, had no real following, and his successor restored the Church to its previous position. In the last half of the century the new religion spread to the Germans (Burgundians, Lombards, Vandals, and the tribes to the east of the Vandals in Map 362), but unfortunately they were converted to Arian Christianity, which, though temporarily in vogue in the Empire, was soon denounced by the hierarchy for its deviationism concerning the nature of the Trinity. This was much debated: was God the Father quite separate from God the Son (the Arian view)? was one merely an aspect of the other (the Sabellian view)? or were they at once distinct and similar? By the time this was settled, the Arians and Sabellians pronounced heretical, and the third idea accepted, a new storm had broken over the relation of the human and divine components of Christ: whether they were com-

pletely fused, entirely separate, or separate but commingled. As before, the mystical compromise was finally adopted, the Monophysite doctrine of complete fusion and the Nestorian of entire separation being condemned after a struggle lasting through the fifth and sixth centuries. The importance of these subtle arguments lies in the adoption of dissenting views as a badge by people at odds with authority or by nations groping for a sense of unity. In those days of pragmatic political thought, an attempt to secede from the Empire on the basis of 'Armenia for the Armenians' would have been unthinkable. But the central power could be indirectly challenged by adopting the local patriotic heresy, and thus the Monophysitism so passionately adhered to in Egypt, Syria (which at first inclined to Nestorianism), and Armenia was really a sign of discontent otherwise inexpressible. The African Donatists could not achieve so subtle a sublimation: in opposing the appointment of a certain bishop of Carthage their insubordination crossed the indefinite boundary between lay and ecclesiastical affairs and they brought down on their heads the full weight of the civil arm. Pelagianism, the native British development, rather lost its point when the legions left and the heathen Saxon became the antagonist, but in its concern with this life rather than the next it seems temporarily to have tapped a deep stream in the insular character.

In contrast, German Arianism was the banner of a proud and very successful minority, fearful of absorption into the mass of Catholics they had subjugated. This attempt to exist as a distinct and superior class was shortsighted, for it was a continual reminder of the narrow base and foreign nature of Gothic rule. Clovis, King of the Franks, owed much of his success over the Visigoths to his shrewd adoption of Catholicism, which enabled him to pose as liberator to the Roman provincials

and their priests. The efficacy of this course was shown on the field of Vouillé, in the persistence and vitality of the Frankish state as a whole, and by the imitation of the Burgundians, who transferred from Arianism to Catholicism in 516.

The Jewish religion won adherents among the Berbers and Arabs at this time, but the only faith which advanced comparably with the Christian was that taught by Mani (215–76), which relates to Mazdaism (the national religion of Persia) rather as does Christianity to Judaism. Manicheism, while accepting the Mazdaist thesis that life is a struggle between the Gods of good and evil, preached an advanced personal ethic having many similarities to the Christian. In spite of repression, it spread rapidly in Persia (though never displacing Mazdaism) and after its introduction into the Roman Empire for a time seemed to be challenging the Christians' newly-won position. But public opinion soon turned against it, and by the sixth century persecution had forced it underground. The Christian counter-invasion of Persia, the work of the Nestorians, never really developed. Each government seems to have been ready to welcome the others' heretics; and if the Manicheans over-exploited their original welcome, turning it into enmity, the Nestorians' survival in Persia can be related to their very limited success.

Nubia and Abyssinia are the only Christian countries not on the map: they were converted in the early sixth and fifth centuries respectively, but lost what little contact they had with the rest of Christendom when the Moslems conquered Egypt (see page 24).

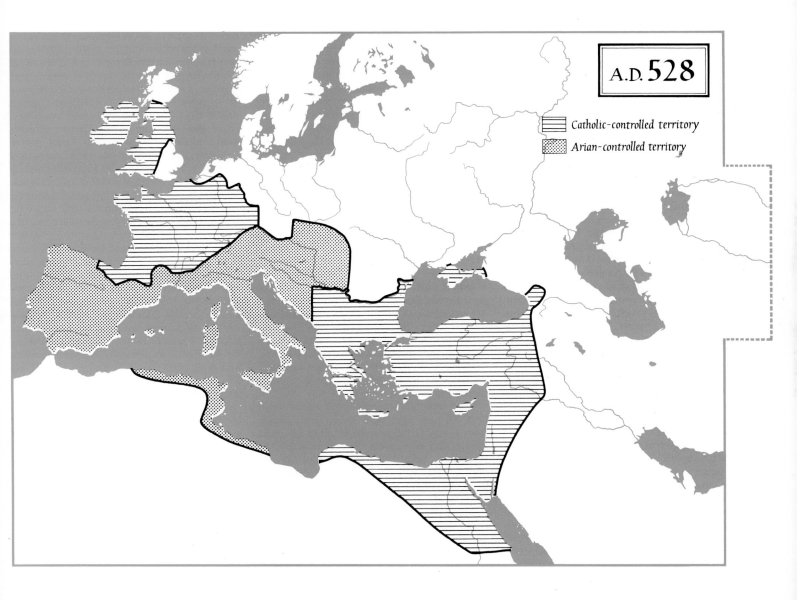

A.D. 528

Catholic-controlled territory
Arian-controlled territory

528 E

This map shows the principal trade routes and towns of the Europe–Near-East area in the early sixth century and the commodities which were produced provincially in exportable surplus. Two trade routes entered the area from outside. The more northerly, the silk route, stretched from China across Central Asia and Persia to the Eastern Roman Empire; the other, the spice route from India, crossed the Indian Ocean and Persian Gulf and joined the silk route in Mesopotamia. The secret of silk-worm culture had gradually seeped across Asia along with the traffic in the product, but the chronology of its spread is very uncertain. At the date of this map, the nature of silk was still obscure to the Eastern Romans. Raw silk and silk goods were, as one might expect, the staple of the silk route; the term spice, however, obscures rather than explains the commodities of the Indian trade. It includes a wide range of goods traded in small amounts, not merely the pepper, cloves, nutmeg, and so on of today, but also dyes, mordants, scents, pigments, gums, incense, and a heterogeneous collection of substances hopefully believed to be of medical value. Spices traversed all routes, but many derived from India and the metropolitan province of Persia. The remaining routes are the Mediterranean network dominated by Constantinople, the Black Sea extension of this, by which trade was carried on with the Huns, and the Red Sea route to Arabia and East Africa.

It will be seen that nearly all the large towns of the time lay on important routes, and of course the relation between trade and town is fundamental and mutually nutritive. To the trader in caravan or ship the town offered a haven of safety where he could exchange or sell goods and restock with necessities. To the townsman the trader was both a source of revenue and an outlet for the products of local agriculture and industry. All towns produced textiles, glass, pottery, and metalwork, and even if there was little difference in essential technique between the products of one town and those of another the more expensive article could be traded at a profit on the idiosyncrasy or excellence of its craftsmanship. There has been no attempt to show such manufactures on the map; they are sufficiently indicated by the presence of a town. They did, however, greatly swell the volume of trade and went far towards giving a route a vitality of its own.

Silk goods and spices, repeatedly mentioned in contemporary sources, give an impression that the Eastern Empire was failing to balance its trade and that its gold reserves were being dissipated to buy frivolities. Yet contemporary sources are often misleading, for captivated by exceptional luxuries of exotic origin – Baltic amber, Arabian emeralds, Indian pearls and diamonds – they neglect the volume of workaday trade. The superior size of the great Eastern Roman cities was probably reflected in a volume of exportable manufactures that easily sufficed to pay for the luxuries imported from Persia, and though it is true that the Eastern Emperors forbade the export of bullion at this time, this was principally due to their military weakness. All available gold was needed for subsidizing friends and placating enemies abroad.

Some important commodities of Roman trade have not been mentioned so far: corn, coming from Egypt, Sicily, and the Crimea; furs from Russia; and slaves from the barbarian borders everywhere. Egypt had a monopoly of papyrus, but papyrus no longer held the unique place it had in the ancient world. Since the beginning of the Christian era, the parchment book had been steadily ousting the papyrus roll.

The paucity of towns and trade in continental Europe at this time has been remarked in the preface. Even Mediterranean traffic had practically come to a stop in the West, though in this case much of the decline was due to the predatory activities of the Vandals. Rome dwindled to a city of the second rank once the supply of African corn dried up, and as the Vandals became less belligerent so they lost control of the interior and became unable where they had formerly been unwilling to renew the flow. Though the Eastern Emperor Justinian conquered the Vandals, he too proved incapable of regaining the valuable inland parts of the province and there was little revival of trade in the western Mediterranean. Justinian's economic policies were intelligent but unrequited. Seeing the stranglehold Persia had on the silk and spice routes, he attempted to divert these further to the north and south respectively. An embassy was sent to the Transoxian Turks to see if the silk traffic could be routed north of the Caspian, while interference in Arabian and Abyssinian affairs was intended to safeguard the Red Sea outlet and encourage the Egyptian merchants to sail round Arabia to India. This they had done in the early days of the Empire, and probably a few Indian goods still passed this way via Arab middlemen. But Egyptian ships plying the Red Sea at this time were only concerned with Sudanese and East-African gold, ivory, and slaves, and with the few spices that these regions and Arabia could provide. Justinian failed in his attempts, for though his ideas were sound – both routes were fully utilized a few centuries later – he could not even begin to control such distant areas as the Volga steppe and Abyssinia. His one unqualified economic success was in obtaining silk-worms by stealth. They were put to work by 550.

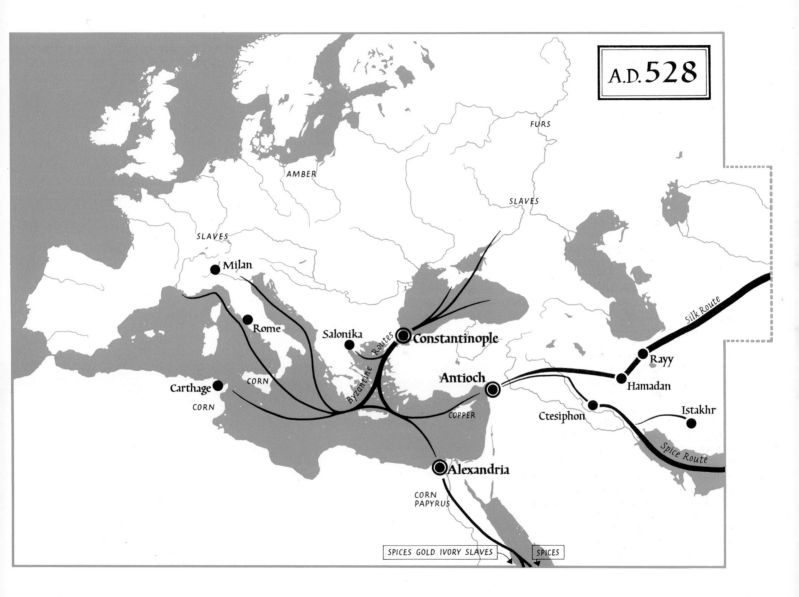

A.D. 528

FURS

AMBER

SLAVES

SLAVES

Milan

Rome

Salonika

Byzantine Routes

Constantinople

Antioch

Silk Route

Rayy

Hamadan

Ctesiphon

Istakhr

Carthage

CORN

CORN

COPPER

Spice Route

Alexandria

CORN
PAPYRUS

SPICES GOLD IVORY SLAVES   SPICES

562

Justinian, who became Emperor in 527, dedicated himself and the Eastern Empire to the reconquest of the West. This required a defensive policy on the Persian frontier, and in spite of almost continual war Persian annexation was limited to Iberia, which was already her vassal. Justinian's military adventure began with an attack on the Vandals, whose kingdom disintegrated with unexpected speed (533), leaving the victor free to turn against the Ostrogoths. Sicily was taken (535) and Italy invaded (536), but after a collapse as rapid as that of the Vandals the Ostrogoths rallied and were not finally crushed until 563, when a second army was sent out by the land route to Italy. In 554 a Visigothic civil war offered an easy occupation of the southern third of Spain. These were remarkable successes; brilliantly served by first class generals, Justinian had achieved a very considerable part of his unrealistic plan. It is fashionable to say that the cost of his victories was too high; that the Eastern homelands had been exhausted to win back provinces that were too devastated to defend themselves. But the restoration of Roman hegemony in the Mediterranean increased the power as well as the prestige of the Empire, as Sancta Sophia and San Vitale represent something more than the whim of a despot.

The four sons of Clovis continued their father's aggrandizement of the Frankish kingdom. Part of Septimania was wrested from the Visigoths (531) and Thuringia was annexed in the same year; Burgundy was subjugated (534) and Provence acquired from the weakening Ostrogoths (536). In 555 the Bavarians, who had moved into modern Bavaria on the collapse of the Ostrogoths, acknowledged Frankish suzerainty. The enlarged Frankish Kingdom came, moreover, under a single rule in 558, by which date all but one of the sons of Clovis had died. The survivor, however, left the Kingdom on his death (561) to his four sons and in their dissensions the first period of Frankish expansion came to an end.

In far Asia, the destruction of a great Mongolian Empire by the revolt of its Turkish vassals (552) led to a westward flight of the vanquished, known to the Chinese as the Jouan Jouan. The Turkish power that was founded by this victory advanced rapidly and its western armies crushed the White Huns in 553. On the defeat of their old enemies the Persians quickly occupied the lands south of the Oxus, loudly claiming the victory as their own. The amalgamated remnants of the Jouan Jouan and the White Huns were known in the West as the Avars. Defeated again by the Turks (559), they moved to the Russian steppe, where Justinian paid them to subjugate the Huns and Slavs who were habitual raiders of the Roman provinces in the Balkans (559–61). Supreme from the Volga to the lower Danube, the Avars turned north and west, subduing the Slavs as they went, till in 562 they came into contact with the Franks on the Elbe. After a century's absence, the Asiatic had returned to Europe.

Some time after 525 the Irish began to colonize Western Scotland; the term Scots, originally an alternative to Irish, soon came to be applied exclusively to these settlers from whom the northern Kingdom eventually took its name.

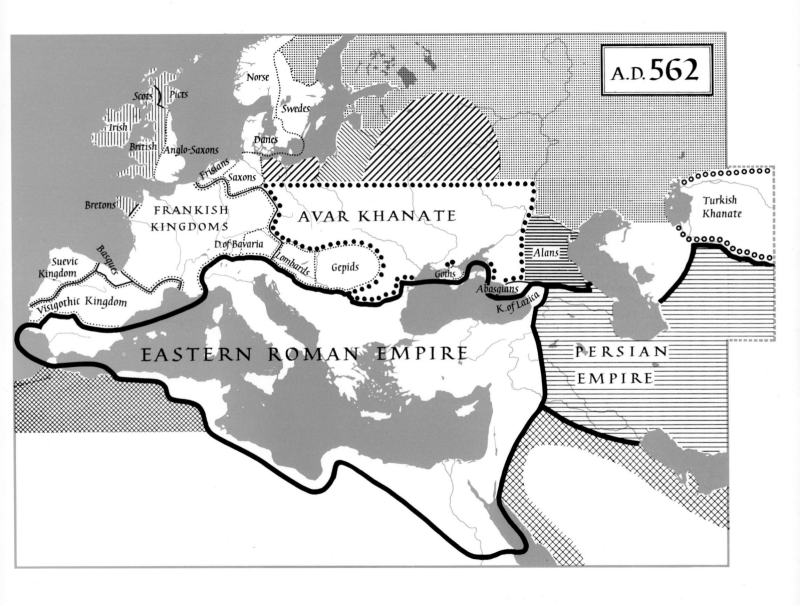

A.D. 562

Norse

Swedes

Scots · Picts

Danes

Irish

British · Anglo-Saxons

Frisians

Bretons

Saxons

FRANKISH KINGDOMS

Basques

D. of Bavaria

Lombards

AVAR KHANATE

Turkish Khanate

Suevic Kingdom

Gepids

Alans

Visigothic Kingdom

Goths

Abasgians

K. of Lazica

EASTERN ROMAN EMPIRE

PERSIAN EMPIRE

600

The Avars wrested Eastern Thuringia from the Franks after a sharp struggle (563), but the vigour of the defence made further Western ventures unattractive. In the east, the invasion of the Caucasus by the Turks (576) seemed to indicate that they were intending to follow their enemies, the Avars, into Europe, but instead their frontier receded again on the division of the Khanate (582). (This Caucasian episode is of importance in that it added a Turkish tribe, the Khazars, to the already heterogeneous population of the region.) The Avar Khan was thus left free to complete the conquest of the Slavs and to intervene in a Lombard–Gepid war which gave him an opportunity to obtain the Hungarian steppe. The Lombards only gained his alliance at the price of their own as well as the Gepid territory. The Gepids annihilated, the Lombards moved off to Italy, and the Avars, as had the Huns before them, centred their Empire on the newly won land (568). The Romans foolishly irritated the Khan by seizing the Gepid town of Belgrade, and although he was unable to expel them until 581 the Khan then took his vengeance on the Balkan provinces. The Romans, fully occupied by a Persian war, were reduced to buying him off.

Fortunately for the Romans, the Persians chose this moment to indulge in internal dissensions, which culminated in the flight of the Persian King, Chosroes II, to the Roman camp. The Emperor Maurice sent him back with an army which regained him his throne; in payment, Chosroes ceded to his benefactor Iberia and nearly all Armenia (591). After this victorious conclusion, Roman troops could be transferred to Europe to restore the Danube defence line and even advance beyond it to chastise the Avars in their homelands.

If Armenia was gained and the Balkans were preserved for the Empire, a considerable part of Italy was lost to the Lombards, who rapidly overran the northern half with the exception of the coasts (568-72) and made Pavia the capital of their new kingdom. A breakthrough to the south resulted in the formation of the Duchies of Spoleto and Benevento (572–82), separated from their theoretical overlord in Pavia by the continuing Imperial control of the Rome–Ravenna corridor. When in 590 a Roman counter-attack cleared the Po valley as far as the gates of Pavia, the new kingdom was itself nearly cut in half, but the Lombards were by no means crushed and the tortuosity of the frontier indicated the uncertainty of the issue. In Spain, too, the Imperial inheritance dwindled. The reviving Visigothic Monarchy reduced the Roman possessions to a coastal strip (575) and by annexing the Suevic Kingdom (584) the Visigoths brought nearly all the peninsula under their control.

32

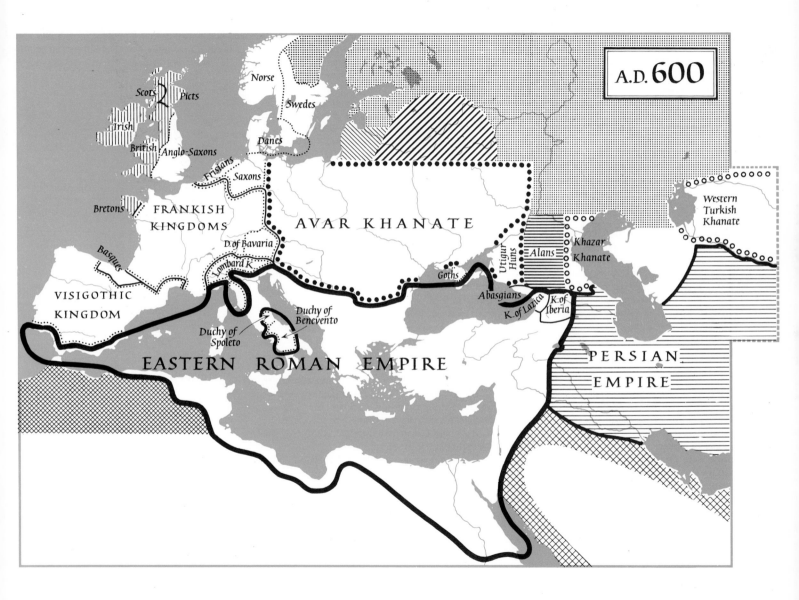

A.D. 600

Norse
Swedes
Scots
Picts
Irish
British
Anglo-Saxons
Danes
Bretons
Frisians
Saxons
FRANKISH
KINGDOMS
D. of Bavaria
Lombard K.
Basques
VISIGOTHIC
KINGDOM
Duchy of
Spoleto
Duchy of
Benevento

AVAR KHANATE

Utigur Huns
Goths
Alans
Khazar
Khanate
Abasgians
K. of Lazica
K. of Iberia

Western
Turkish
Khanate

EASTERN ROMAN EMPIRE

PERSIAN
EMPIRE

626

In 602 the Roman army fighting the Avars revolted, marched on Constantinople, and murdered the Emperor Maurice; the Empire rapidly came to pieces in the hands of the incompetent soldier who was raised to the throne in his place. The Avars devastated the Balkans, left defenceless by the rebellion, though their attention was distracted periodically by trouble with their Slav vassals. In the East, Chosroes II of Persia, who had learnt from the Romans how to profit from dynastic strife, declared his intention of avenging his late benefactor, Maurice. Previous Persian offensives had been a matter of raiding in strength; but Chosroes embarked on an organized conquest of the Eastern provinces. The fortresses of Roman Mesopotamia were reduced (607–15), while Armenia was reoccupied and Anatolia invaded. In 616 Egypt fell to the Persians and the Eastern provinces remaining to the Romans were so ravaged that Heraclius, who had become Emperor in 610, considered centring the Empire anew on the untouched lands in Africa. However, he managed to maintain his position in the East without further loss for the next ten years, towards the end of that time beginning a counter-attack in alliance with the Khazars. With nice strategic insight, he refused to waste his resources on attritive attempts to regain ruined territories, but, marching through Lazica and Iberia, descended on the Persian homeland (623–4). The Persians reacted by attacking Constantinople in alliance with the Avars (626), but their forces were prevented from uniting by the continuing Roman control of the sea, and the Avar assault on the land walls of the capital was repelled. Unable to defend his own capital from Heraclius's army, Chosroes was deposed and murdered by his nobles, who sued for peace while still in possession of half the East (628). Though the evacuation of conquered territories was not complete until 629, that year saw the frontiers restored. Heraclius then completely overhauled the administration of the Empire, the character and language of which had become increasingly Greek in the last half century. In recognition of this renovation, the Empire is at this point renamed Byzantine by historians, Byzantion being the old Greek name for Constantinople.

The Avar power had been declining throughout the opening years of the century. The Slavs on the Elbe and in Bohemia repudiated Avar suzerainty (605?), and the numerous Slav tribes who had moved into the depopulated areas of the Balkans could not be effectively dominated. Following the Avar failure before Constantinople in 626, these attained complete independence. The Huns also seceded and, Utigurs and Kutrigurs coalescing, formed a united Khanate in the Azov region. The name 'Hun' was exchanged for that of Bulgar, and the new nation became known as Great Bulgaria.

In Western Europe events were on a smaller scale. The Frankish kingdom, united again in 613, was finally divided in a manner which is geographically and not merely genealogically valid. The kingdoms of Neustria and Austrasia, as defined at their separation in 623, have a continuity which is distinct from the previous disconnected and fluctuating partitions. In Spain, the Visigoths further reduced the Byzantine possessions (612); in Italy, the Lombards regained control of the northern plain (601–5).

The Anglo–Saxon conquest of England was a slow if thorough process hampered in the south by the number of their petty kings. The north, invaded later, was overrun much more rapidly, and it was here in Northumbria that the first considerable Anglo–Saxon kingdom was established. Under Northumbrian leadership, the tempo of the advance quickened and the western coast was reached at two points. The British of Wales were thus cut off from their weaker kin-folk in Strathclyde (to the north) and Cornwall (to the south).

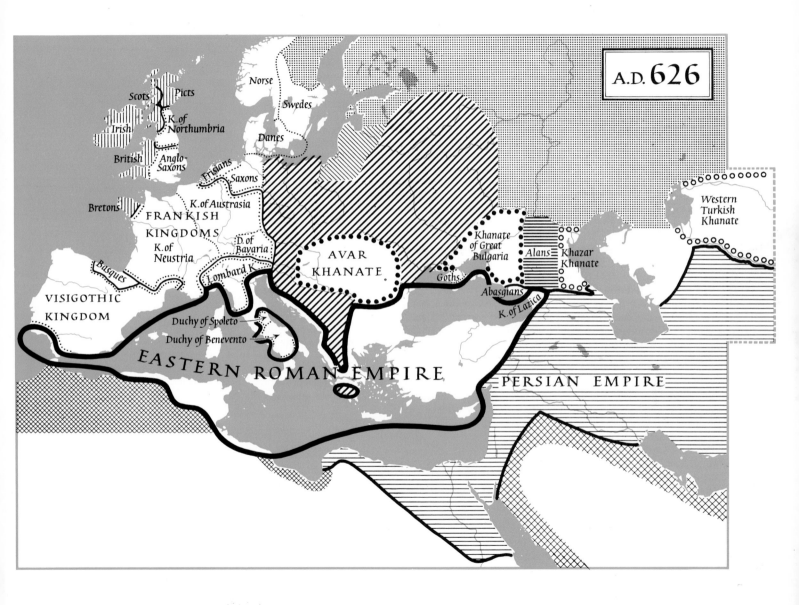

A.D. 626

Scots · Picts
Irish
K. of Northumbria
British · Anglo-Saxons
Norse
Swedes
Danes
Bretons
Frisians
Saxons
FRANKISH KINGDOMS
K. of Austrasia
K. of Neustria
D. of Bavaria
Basques
Lombard K.
VISIGOTHIC KINGDOM
Duchy of Spoleto
Duchy of Benevento
AVAR KHANATE
Goths
Khanate of Great Bulgaria
Alans
Abasgians
K. of Lazica
Khazar Khanate
Western Turkish Khanate
EASTERN ROMAN EMPIRE
PERSIAN EMPIRE

650

While the Byzantine and Persian Empires had been engaged in their fruitless and costly war, the Arabs had been politically and spiritually united by Mohammed. To the great Empires, the affairs of Arabia were of little interest; they protected their frontiers from marauders by subsidizing the nearest chieftains, a measure which had always been adequate before. But though, as might have been predicted, the unity imposed by Mohammed died with him (632), Islam lived on to recreate his temporal rule and extend it beyond the horizon of the Prophet. By 634 Arabia had been re-united and the first armies dispatched. Heraclius watched while the provinces he had won back were lost again. But the Arabs did not rest content with Syria, Egypt, and Mesopotamia (conquered 636-8, 640-2, and 639-46 respectively), but seized Tripolitania (642) and were with difficulty repulsed from Tunisia. The old Emperor, as he heard of the loss of Genoa to the Lombards (640) and of the last Imperial possessions in Spain to the Visigoths (631), must have felt that his life's work had been in vain.

His erstwhile enemies, the Persians, may well have considered him fortunate. Their Empire was completely overrun (637-49) and, apart from a few nobles who maintained their independence in the mountains of Tabaristan, the ancient Persian state became a fief of Islam. The Persian inheritance included the enmity of the Turks on the Oxus and of the Khazars in Transcaucasia. The collapse of the Western Turkish Khanate in 630, prevented the Turks from exploiting the Persian disasters and the Arabs at first contented themselves with the Persian frontiers. But the Khazars were expanding rapidly and *circa* 650 they defeated their Caucasian opponents, the Alans and the Bulgars.[1] The southward expansion of the new power conflicted with the northern drive of the Arabs and led to a three-cornered war between Khazars, Arabs, and Byzantines in Armenia, which endowed that country with the spurious independence of a no-man's land. Cyprus, from which both Arabs and Byzantines exacted tribute, was in a similarly ill-defined and unhappy state.

The successors of Mohammed, the Caliphs, combined, as he had, the powers of Emperor and Pope and were at first elected. The third Caliph, Uthman (644–56), of the aristocratic family of the Umayyads, laid the foundations for a hereditary Caliphate by extensive nepotism. He gained the ultimate essential – popular support – by being murdered, and though the new Caliph Ali was the son-in-law of the Prophet, he was unable to break the power of the Umayyads. They regained the Caliphate on his death (661) and held it for the next century. The matter is of more than dynastic moment, for the feeling, nurtured by the opposition to the Umayyads, that Ali and his descendants were the rightful heirs of the Prophet became incorporated in the religious dogma of the discontented factions. The schism between the Orthodox (Sunnite) and Alid (Shiite) Islam is important today, when the Umayyads are no more than a strain on one's spelling.

In Britain the primacy was taken from Northumbria by the midland Kingdom of Mercia (642), to which the rest of the Anglo–Saxon kingdoms then became subject.

---

1. Some of the Bulgars fled to the Danube; some up the Volga; the Volga Bulgars remained under Khazar suzerainty.

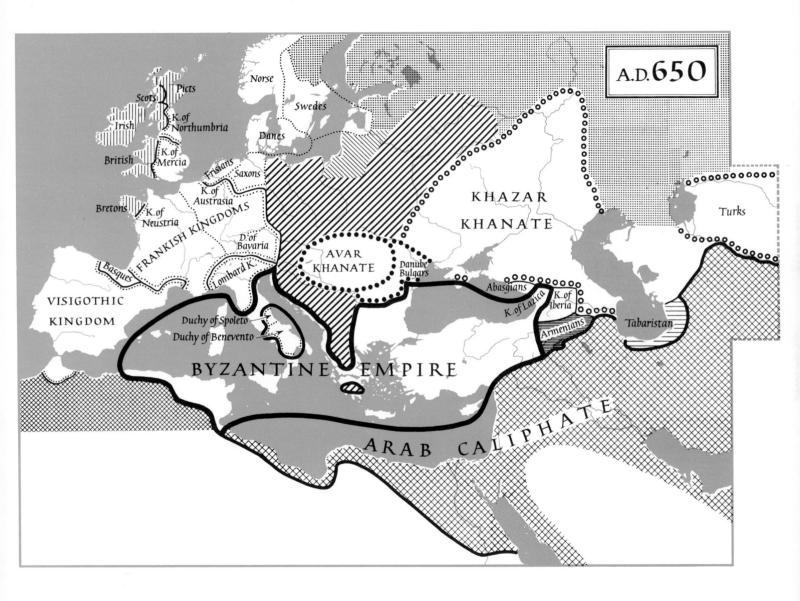

A.D. 650

Picts
Scots
K. of
Northumbria
Irish
British
K. of
Mercia
Bretons
K. of
Neustria
Norse
Swedes
Danes
Frisians
Saxons
K. of
Austrasia
FRANKISH KINGDOMS
Basques
D. of
Bavaria
Lombard K.
VISIGOTHIC
KINGDOM
Duchy of Spoleto
Duchy of Benevento
BYZANTINE EMPIRE
AVAR
KHANATE
Danube
Bulgars
KHAZAR
KHANATE
Turks
Abasgians
K. of Lazica
K. of
Iberia
Tabaristan
Armenians
ARAB CALIPHATE

737

The first flood of Islam had spent itself by 650 and, although there was rarely peace on the frontiers of the new state, the next half century did not bring advances on the previous epic scale. The Byzantines, holding a shorter line than before, counter-attacked in Asia Minor and hung on grimly in Tunisia. But the conversion of the Berbers gave renewed force to Islam in Africa, and in 696 the Byzantine provinces there were overrun. The conquerors swept on into Spain, and the defeat of the Visigoths (711) delivered the whole peninsula, with the exception of a northern strip,[1] to the Arabs. The invaders also took over the Visigothic corner of France and began to enlarge it energetically. The Franks had however been reunited by an able line of Mayors of the Palace who, ruling on behalf of the impotent descendants of Clovis, restored to the realm the vigour of its earlier days. In 732 the Mayor Charles Martel inflicted on the Arabs a defeat sufficiently decisive to end their threat to France, though the Arab raids continued on a reduced scale for some years.

On its central and eastern fronts the Caliphate took a little longer to get its second wind. The final conquest of Armenia, Iberia, and Lazica was not achieved till 717; this success was followed up by a devastating invasion of the Khazar homelands (737), which put an end to the greatness of the Khanate.[2] But the great sea-borne attack on Constantinople (717–18) failed miserably, and the Byzantines remained unconquered. Their line in Anatolia was slowly pushed back however and in the Balkans they were forced to cede land to the rising power of the Danube Bulgars (679). The political consequences of the end of Byzantine rule in central Italy and the western Mediterranean – the aggrandizement of the Lombard Kingdom, the independence of Naples, Amalfi, and Venice, and the emergence of the

Papal States – are apparent on this map. What became of Corsica and Sardinia is obscure.

The divisions and dissensions of the Turks made eastward expansion comparatively easy for the Arabs, but again it was not till the early eighth century that any considerable territory was reduced, and then, as in Africa, the conquests were due to the energy of the local Emir (Governor) rather than the direction of the Caliphate. The Caliphs themselves were prepared to tolerate the practical independence of the highland aristocracy of Tabaristan, much nearer home.

In Britain, the Kingdom of Northumbria regained the leadership of the Anglo–Saxons (655) and reduced to vassalage the Welsh (as the British had come to be called) of Strathclyde, the Picts, and the Scots. But this revival was brief and even before the Picts and Scots threw off the Northumbrian yoke (695) the other Anglo–Saxon Kingdoms had transferred their allegiance to Mercia (679).

1. This contained the inevitably independent Basques and the Kingdom of the Asturias, which had a tenuous claim to be the heir of the Visigoths.
2. The Volga Bulgars took advantage of the Khazar defeats and asserted their independence; the same is probably true of the Magyars, a Finnish tribe that had migrated to the Steppe and become the main instrument of Khazar dominion in south Russia. The three powers remained friendly, however, with the Khazars being accorded some degree of seniority.

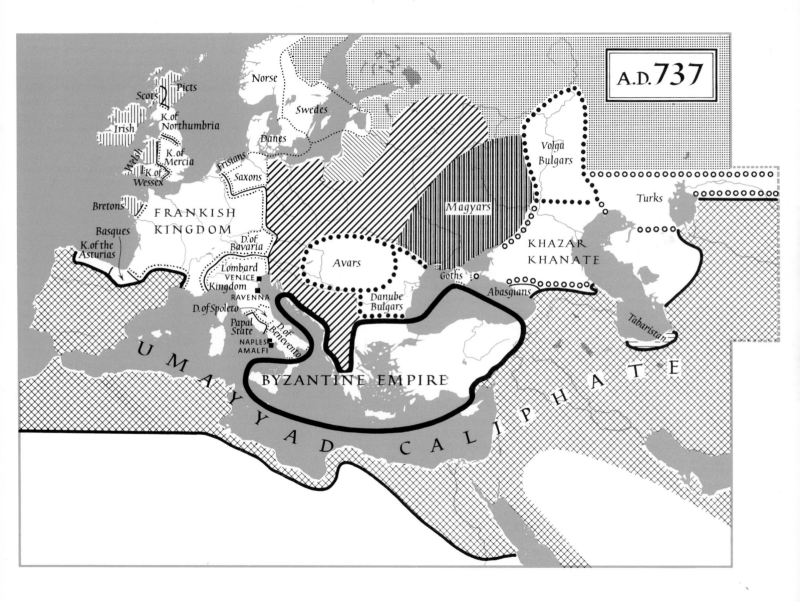

A.D. 737

Scots Picts
Irish K. of Northumbria
Welsh K. of Mercia
K. of Wessex
Bretons Frisians
Basques Saxons
K. of the Asturias
FRANKISH KINGDOM

Norse
Swedes
Danes

Volga Bulgars
Magyars
Turks

D. of Bavaria
Lombard Kingdom VENICE
RAVENNA
D. of Spoleto
Papal State D. of Benevento
NAPLES
AMALFI

Avars
Danube Bulgars
Goths
Abasgians

KHAZAR KHANATE

Tabaristan

BYZANTINE EMPIRE

U M A Y Y A D   C A L I P H A T E

737 R The little affection in which Syria, Armenia, and Egypt held the rule of Constantinople was obvious in the ease with which they fell to the Persians. When he had regained them for the Empire, Heraclius attempted to conciliate their Monophysitism by promulgating a compromise doctrine, Monotheletism, which suggested that the union of God and Man in Christ, though not submerging the identity of either component, was sufficiently complete to manifest itself outwardly in one divine–human energy. Monotheletism did nothing to reconcile the schismatic provinces and indeed it was hopeless to expect a radical cure when only the symptom was being treated. Moreover it irritated the rest of the Empire, so, when the Monophysite area was overrun by the Moslems and Monotheletism lost its meaning, it was quietly abandoned.

Originally the Christian Church had been organized in five Patriarchates: Rome, Constantinople, Antioch, Jerusalem, and Alexandria, among which Rome had always claimed a seniority allowed by the others but regarded by them as without much practical significance. The ultimate religious authority was in fact wielded by the Emperors. After the Arab conquest of Antioch, Jerusalem, and Alexandria their patriarchates fell to the second rank. With only Constantinople and Rome left in the ring, Rome's claim that its pre-eminence implied authority over the whole church became practical politics. Rome cleverly linked her cause with a campaign against Imperial direction of religious affairs.

The fall of the West had freed the Pope from subordination to an Emperor and it had made his parish international. When Justinian re-occupied Rome he proceeded to depose a Pope who did not toe the Imperial line, and it looked as though the old days had returned. But the bulk of the Roman see, and therefore of Papal activity, still lay outside the Empire, and the Papacy kept much of the autonomy it had gained. As the distance between Constantinople and Rome further reduced the possibility of interference, the Pope did not have to follow the twists of Imperial diplomacy as did the Patriarch of Constantinople. In consequence the comparatively unwavering course of the Papacy made it appear even to the East a truer fount of religion than the Patriarchate that functioned as a state department.

During the Byzantine period following the Lombard invasion, the Emperor's hold on central Italy gradually slipped, and the almost isolated Pope assumed the temporal rule of Rome and its environs as an Imperial officer. He thus achieved effective freedom without open rupture. That came when the iconoclastic (image-breaking) decrees of the Emperor Leo III gave the Pope a chance to attain his second objective, control over the Eastern Church. It was in 727 that the Emperor, shamed by the iconophobe and monotheistic Moslems, commanded the destruction of religious pictures and statues, then so numerous and so venerated in his dominions as to be in effect the idols of polytheism. The issue was one on which the West, where images were not overvenerated and iconoclasm therefore not understood, and the East, where images were excessively adored, could be united under the banner of the Papacy in opposition to the Emperor and his puppet patriarch. Leo III was excommunicated and the icons put under papal protection, but the whole scheme rather misfired. In the first place the autocracy in the East proved strong enough to carry out the iconoclastic decrees in spite of all opposition, so that the area recognizing Papal supremacy did not increase (in fact it diminished when the south-Italian districts over which the Byzantines retained control were transferred to the Patriarchate of Constantinople); in the second, although Central Italy was solidly for the Pope and the Byzantine attempt at reconquest failed, in the confusion the Lombards overran all of it except Venice, an island confederacy, and Rome and the area round it. The Pope allied himself with the Venetians in an attempt to win back central Italy 'for the Empire', that is as a province to be returned when iconoclasm had been renounced and the papal primacy accepted, but the Venetians could only retake Ravenna and that was lost again around 750. By then it was obvious that the main bid had failed; with the Eastern Church firmly under Byzantine control the Pope was left as temporal Lord of an estate too small to be viable in a Lombard environment. The Venetians, following their commercial instincts, accepted a nominal imperial suzerainty which safeguarded their trading at Constantinople and left them free in other matters, such as continuing to be part of the Roman see.

In general this map shows a shrinkage of Christendom due to the advance of Islam, while internally the elimination of Arianism by conquest (Ostrogoths and Vandals) or conversion to Catholicism (Lombards, 653, Visigoths, 589) is more than counterbalanced by the East–West split. By Frankish conquest, Christianity was brought to the Thuringians and Bavarians; by Irish and Roman evangelism, to the Picts (sixth century) and the Anglo–Saxons of England (seventh century). The Irish Church, cut off from Rome by the barbarian invasions shortly after its foundation (fifth century), at first resisted reabsorption into the Roman see, but ultimately acquiesced. These were small successes to set against the loss of Africa, Syria, and Spain.

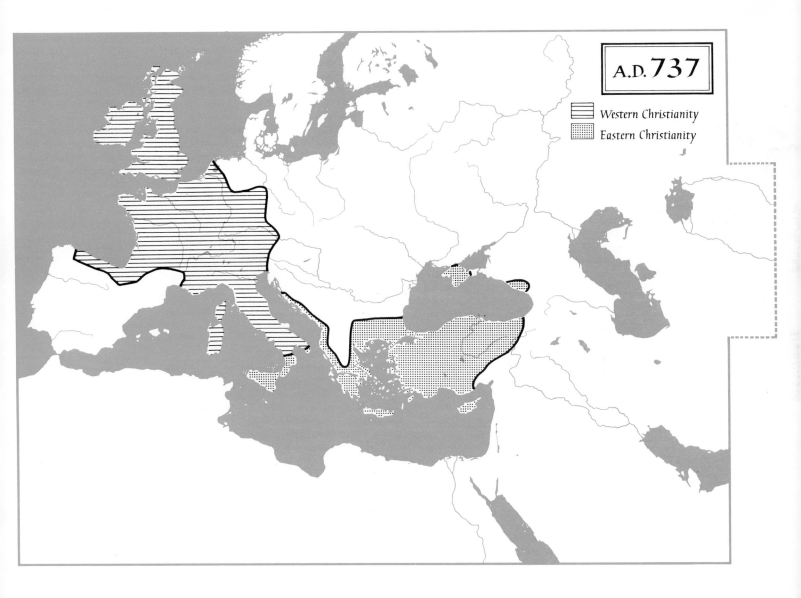

A.D. 737

Western Christianity
Eastern Christianity

Islam, at least at first, brought unity and peace to an area comparable in size to the Roman Empire, and it was natural that trade and civilization should flower in such an environment. But whereas the Roman Empire had the Mediterranean as a centre, the Arab Empire occupied a solid land mass. Seas lapped its edges, but its trade was largely overland. The great Roman ports declined and the new cities that arose were never on the sea. To such an extent did the Arabs ignore the shipping routes that caravans even plied between Egypt and Tunisia along the barren coast of North Africa. Considering the relative cost of land and sea transport, this is eloquent of the failure of the Caliphate to pacify even its coastal waters. The Arabs were good sailors – the trade routes from India flourished in their hands and their piracy severely damaged Byzantine trade – yet they failed to utilize the seas around them. The outlook of the Arab, accustomed to long desert journeys, seems responsible for this. It exaggerated the tendency of the East to trade mainly in luxury goods, for only the small and costly can be economically transported overland.

Justinian's projects for the opening of new routes came to fruition in Arab times. With Persia, Arabia, and Egypt under one rule, there was no obstacle to the shipment of Indian and Arabian spices direct to Egypt; Egypt in return exported to Arabia the corn that no longer went to Constantinople. Not the Arabs but the Khazars bringing peace to south Russia made possible the realization of Justinian's other idea: the rerouting of Asian trade north of the Caspian.[1] This brought some compensation to the Byzantines for the loss of so much elsewhere; as Mediterranean trade shrank, the Black Sea traffic expanded. The Byzantine resources were, however, gravely depleted, and it was an achievement to survive. The loss of

Egypt meant not only a shortage of corn, but of gold; and the iconoclastic movement was probably partly motivated by the necessity of tapping the Church's accumulation of precious metal.

The trade of north-west Europe occupies a very minor position in these first two economic maps, as though it had ceased with the disappearance of the last Roman ship from the Atlantic (422). But commercial activity, mainly in Frisian hands, was considerable, wine, salt, and oil being traded as well as the usual manufactures (glass, textiles, metalwork). A few Byzantine goods percolated through the Alps or Southern France and in return the West sent slaves, iron, and timber to the East.

This is perhaps a convenient moment to survey the textiles of the medieval period as a whole. There are four naturally occurring fibres which can be woven into cloth. The most glamorous, silk, has already been discussed, while flax, from which linen is made, grows almost anywhere. The use of wool was also universal, but the north-west of Europe probably always produced a better quality and soon began to export woollen goods. Cotton growing was confined to the Near East. It was introduced to Spain and Italy by the Moslems, but never spread further and there was little demand for it in the cold North. Of the dyes available, the ones extracted from plants (woad, saffron, and madder) were common to all countries; the litmus lichen grew only in the north. By far the best dyes were those derived from insects of the Coccidae family. The most famous today is cochineal, but this comes from the New World, and other species furnished the kermes (carmine) of Spain and the Near East (particularly Anatolia and Transcaucasia) and the lac of India.[2] To vary the effects possible with such a small number of dyes and to render them more brilliant and durable, mordants (usually alums) were necessary.

Alums were obtained principally from the Sahara via Egypt and Morocco and from Anatolia. At the end of the thirteenth century, the Genoese gained complete control of the market, obtaining their supplies from rich mines in western Anatolia. By that time the synthesis of alum (from aluminium sulphate and wine) had been achieved by Arab chemists, but the process never achieved commercial importance. When the Turks occupied Anatolia Europe was only saved from an alum famine by the discovery of extensive deposits of alunite (a mineral closely related and easily transformed to alum) in the Papal States. Papal alum factories started production in the middle of the fifteenth century and the Papacy long held a monopoly in alum thereafter.

1. Though south of the Aral – not north as in Justinian's trial.

2. India also exported a logwood dye.

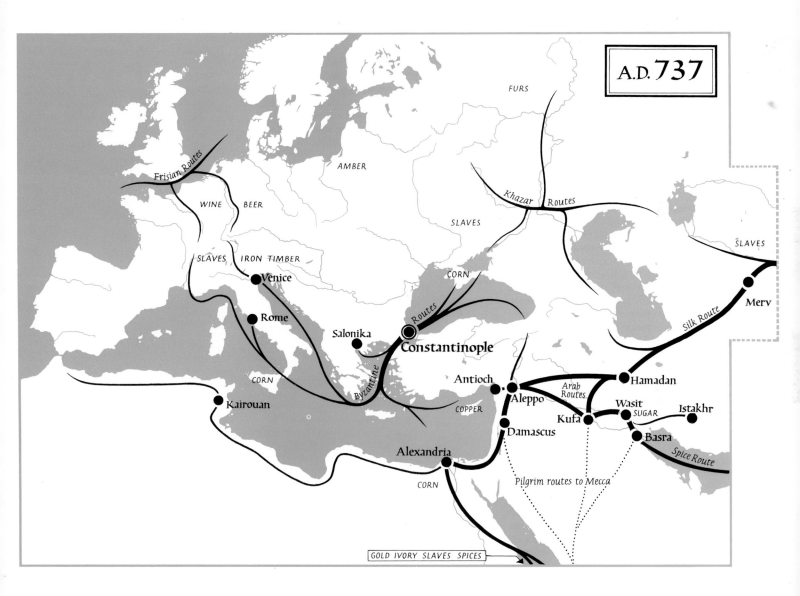

A.D. 737

FURS

AMBER

Frisian Routes

WINE   BEER

Khazar Routes

SLAVES

SLAVES

SLAVES   IRON TIMBER

CORN

Venice

Rome

Salonika

Silk Route

Merv

CORN

Routes

◎ **Constantinople**

Byzantine

Antioch

Hamadan

CORN

Kairouan

COPPER

Aleppo

Arab Routes

Wasit

Istakhr

Kufa

SUGAR

Damascus

Basra

Alexandria

Spice Route

CORN

Pilgrim routes to Mecca

GOLD IVORY SLAVES SPICES →

771

In 749 political and religious discontent with Umayyad rule suddenly blazed out into open rebellion, but apart from the massacre of the Umayyad family which they prosecuted with vigour the rebels had few aims in common. The result was no more than a change of dynasty, the Abbasids, in whom the Caliphate now became hereditary, declaring for Orthodox Islam in spite of the crucial support they had received from the Shiites. The decline that had begun under the later Umayyads continued under the Abbasids; the fanaticism that had insisted on world conquest disappeared and, though prosperous and powerful, the Caliphate ceased to expand.[1] The Umayyads had governed from Damascus, leaving to the Arabian capital of Mecca only its religious predominance; the Abbasids founded a new city, Baghdad (763), from which to rule their territories; and, increasingly influenced by the Persian culture which surrounded them, they lost touch with the Arabic and Moorish components of Islam. However the only province which actually refused to recognize the early Abbasids was Spain. There, one of the few Umayyads to survive founded an independent state (756) after a bitter struggle which gave the Christians of northern Spain the chance to win back Galicia and refound their Kingdom on a surer basis.

After taking Ravenna from the Venetians (c. 750) the Lombards prepared to absorb the unintentionally independent and apparently helpless Papal State. But the Pope, as head of Western Christendom, appealed to the Franks to protect his temporal dominion. The Mayor Pépin II, son of Charles Martel, agreed to help when the Pope sanctioned the deposition of the last of the puppet-kings of the house of Clovis and the elevation of Pépin to the Frankish throne. The Lombards were defeated; and Pépin preserved as a Frankish dependency a Papal State which the Pope persuaded him to enlarge to the size of the erstwhile Byzantine province (756–9).

A minor though significant incident is the establishment by the Bavarian Duchy (which since 638 had been virtually unaware of its allegiance to the Franks) of a protectorate over the Slavs on its eastern border, the beginning of a movement that was to drive a wedge between the southern Slavs and the main mass of their kin (758).

1. Tabaristan, however, was annexed in 765.

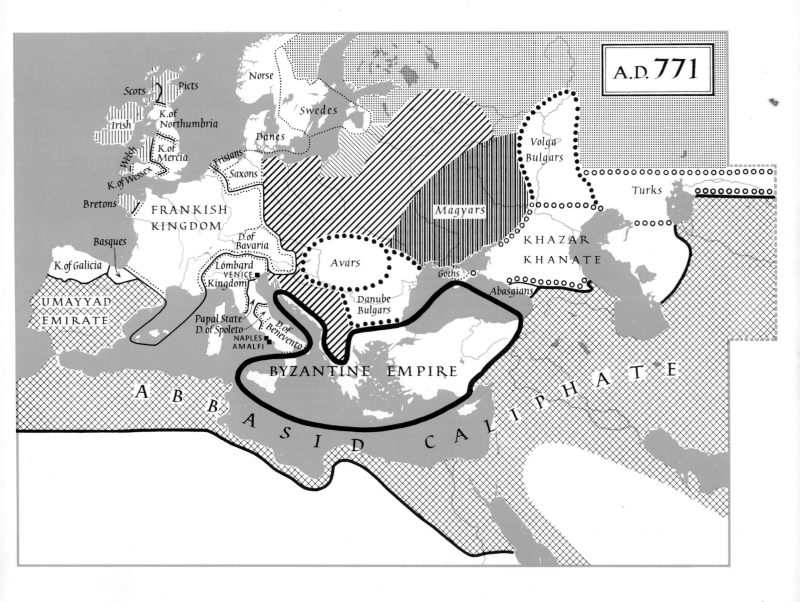

A.D. 771

Scots
Picts
Irish
K. of
Northumbria
Welsh
K. of
Mercia
K. of Wessex
Bretons
Basques
K. of Galicia
UMAYYAD
EMIRATE

Norse
Swedes
Danes
Frisians
Saxons
FRANKISH
KINGDOM
D. of
Bavaria
Lombard
VENICE
Kingdom
Papal State
D. of Spoleto
D. of
Beneveto
NAPLES
AMALFI

Avars

Danube
Bulgars

Magyars

Goths

Volga
Bulgars

Turks

KHAZAR
KHANATE

Abasgians

BYZANTINE EMPIRE

A B B A S I D   C A L I P H A T E

830

Charlemagne, the son of Pépin, who became sole King of the Franks in 771, spent his long reign fighting continual aggressive wars. He annexed the Lombard Kingdom, which had started to nibble at the Pope's estates again, together with the Duchy of Spoleto (774); though the Duchy of Benevento emphasized its independence by elevating itself to a principality. In 778 the Duchy of Bavaria was absorbed into the Frankish Kingdom and Charlemagne intensified the Bavarian policy of establishing protectorates over the neighbouring Slavs. The Avars, the only power who might have opposed this, were far gone in decline. They were destroyed by a combined Frankish and Bulgarian attack (796), and though the Bulgars took over the larger part of the Avar territory they did not trouble the Slav areas under Frankish rule (which included Bohemia, Moravia, Austria, and Croatia). Charlemagne's offensive against the Umayyad Emirate was only minimally successful, though the strip of northern Spain acquired (802) was a buffer against possible Moslem revival. The hardest fighting of this second period of Frankish expansion was against the Saxons, who were only overcome after repeated campaigns (782–804); the elimination of the Frisians, who had lost half their land to the Franks a century before (689), rounds off the list of his conquests. By his personal energy Charlemagne had brought under single rule an area which, if it corresponded to the ancient Empire of the West in size rather than position, was ample justification for his reviving the title of Emperor (800). Even after his death (814), the momentum he had imparted to his creation disguised for a while its lack of governmental machinery; in fact at first it continued to grow. But the voluntary entry into the Empire of the Bretons and of Sardinia[1] was due to the savage piracy that was devastating the North Sea and Mediterranean coasts.

Raiding in the Mediterranean represented the last wave of the original Islamic flood, but it was not directed by the Abbasid Caliphate, whose temporal power was waning fast. The more distant Emirates tended to become independent and hereditary, as in Tunisia (ruled after 800 by the Aghlabid dynasty) and Eastern Persia (ruled after 820 by the Tahirid dynasty), while the Idrisids of Morocco rejected even the spiritual authority of Baghdad, founding a Shiite Caliphate (789). In territory under their direct rule, the Abbasid Caliphs were incapable of vigorous leadership; as early as 788, they lost Lazica to the Abasgians and with it the chance of expansion via the Black Sea. The Western Moslem states on the other hand not only terrorized the Mediterranean but aimed at the possession of its islands. The Umayyads began the reduction of the Balearic Islands (798), the Aghlabids that of Sicily (827), while Crete was overrun by Moslems from Spain (823).

In the North Sea, the raiders were Scandinavians making their explosive entry into European history. The advance of the Frankish frontier had brought the Danes into contact with Western Christendom and the demise of the Frisians had left the North Sea a power vacuum; but the fury that these events appeared to release was the result of Scandinavian over-population troubles, which skill in navigation made exportable. The westward raiding of the Vikings (Danes and Norwegians) was mirrored in the East by the passage of the Varangians (Danes and Swedes) along the great rivers of Russia. The Swedes had been colonizing the Russian shore of the Baltic for more than a century; now principalities were erected at Novgorod and Kiev, in the heart of the Slav territory, while the establishment of a Black Sea stronghold at Tmutorokan (825) challenged the Khazar control of the Don-to-Constantinople trade. The success of these interior ventures led

to the abandonment of the less profitable Scandinavian colonies in the Gulf of Riga.

As the time approached when the Vikings too would graduate from piracy to conquest, the Frankish Empire displayed the disadvantages of a unity beyond its means and the British Isles the opposite perils of division. The state of the Anglo-Saxons was improved, however, by the rise of the Kingdom of Wessex, which overcame the Cornish Welsh and the southern dependencies of Mercia (825) and then enforced the submission of both Mercia and Northumbria (829).

---

1. Corsica had passed to the Franks in 774, the Balearic Islands twenty years before that.

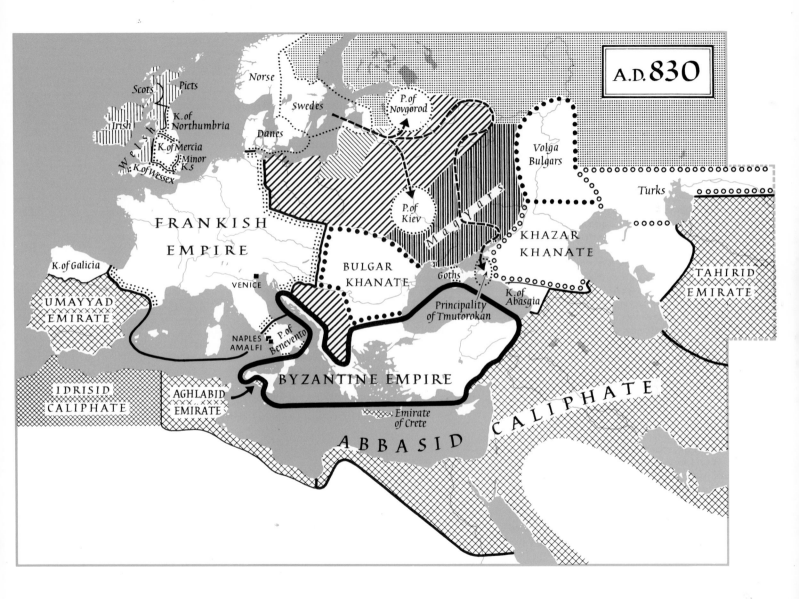

A.D. 830

Scots
Picts
Irish
K. of
Northumbria
Welsh
K. of Mercia
Minor
Ks
K. of Wessex

Norse
Swedes
Danes

P. of
Novgorod

Volga
Bulgars

Turks

P. of
Kiev

Magyars

KHAZAR
KHANATE

FRANKISH
EMPIRE

K. of Galicia

VENICE

BULGAR
KHANATE

Goths

K. of
Abasgia

Principality
of Tmutorokan

TAHIRID
EMIRATE

UMAYYAD
EMIRATE

NAPLES
AMALFI

P. of
Benevento

BYZANTINE EMPIRE

IDRISID
CALIPHATE

AGHLABID
EMIRATE

Emirate
of Crete

ABBASID   CALIPHATE

888

In 843 the Frankish Empire was divided between the three grandsons of Charlemagne, and in the next forty years there was a kaleidoscopic series of partitions and amalgamations reflecting Carolingian reproduction and mortality. Historians describe these divisions as significant when they correspond to modern frontiers and stigmatize them as typically dynastic when they do not, but by 885 a series of accidents had reunited the Empire, and it was in 887–8 that the definitive disintegration took place. The main successor kingdoms were France, Germany, and Italy; in addition, ambitious nobles carved out the minor kingdoms of Provence and Jurane Burgundy, the Bretons and Basques reverted to their traditional independence, and the County of Barcelona became practically independent. The Frankish authority over the middle European Slavs largely collapsed; in its place arose the native Kingdom of Great Moravia.

During the same period the Abbasid Caliphate continued its own slower devolution. The eastern Emirates passed into the possession of the Samanid (874) and Saffarid (867) dynasties which represented a national Persian revival; Egypt became independent under the Tulunid Emirs and Christian Armenia received autonomy at the price of tribute.[1] The weakness of the Caliphate even forced it to tolerate the establishment of a descendant of Ali in Tabaristan under the protection of the pro-Shiite Saffarids (885). In the Mediterranean the Aghlabids practically completed their conquest of Sicily and from 840 to 880 held the heel of Italy. They were expelled by combined Byzantine–Frankish efforts, of which the Byzantines gained the profit. It was their first territorial gain for two centuries and their possession of it was assured more by the political disunity and impoverished state of the peninsula[2] than by the force of Imperial arms. What resources the Byzantines possessed were needed in the Balkans where the Bulgars were expanding rapidly, though mainly at the expense of the Slavs.

The ravages of the Vikings were distributed over the whole of the area within their reach, but the British Isles were the object of their attempts at conquest. The Norsemen overran the islands and the north and west shores of Scotland, the Danes the centre two thirds of England. But in each case the invaders stimulated their prey into unity, Kenneth MacAlpin uniting the Picts and Scots (844),[3] and Alfred of Wessex, the only intact English Kingdom, fighting for the whole English nation. When in 878 Alfred recaptured London, the chances of Danish rule in England faded.[4]

The Russian Principalities founded by the Varangians were united by Oleg (880), and the expansion of the vast new state proceeded the more rapidly for the defeat of the Magyars by the Patzinak Turks (c. 860). The Patzinak invasion drove a wedge between the Khazars and their junior partners, the Magyars and the Volga Bulgars, and ended the Khazar control of the Russian steppe. In the ensuing struggle between the nomad Turks and the Russian Principality for the possession of South Russia, the Khazars played an increasingly unimportant part, though they do not finally disappear until about 1030.

---

1. This revived Kingdom of Armenia included within its boundaries the old Georgian Kingdom of Iberia. Its northern capital, Tiflis, remained in Arab hands.

2. The (North) Italian Kingdom was disputed between Berengar of Friuli and Guy of Spoleto and fully possessed by neither; the Principality of Benevento was split into three (Benevento, Capua, and Salerno), and the seaports of Naples, Amalfi, and Venice, though nominally Byzantine, were actually independent.

3. Strathclyde became a dependency of the Kingdom of Scotland in 908, and was formally absorbed into it in 945.

4. The history of Scandinavia itself is very fragmentary before the tenth century, but the Norwegian Kingdom would seem to have been founded c. 885. At that time the Danes were disunited and perhaps dependent on Sweden, whose monarchy seems to be the oldest of the three. Temporary unity was certainly achieved in both Denmark and Sweden under Heroic Kings long before this date, but the extent and chronology of their rule is problematical.

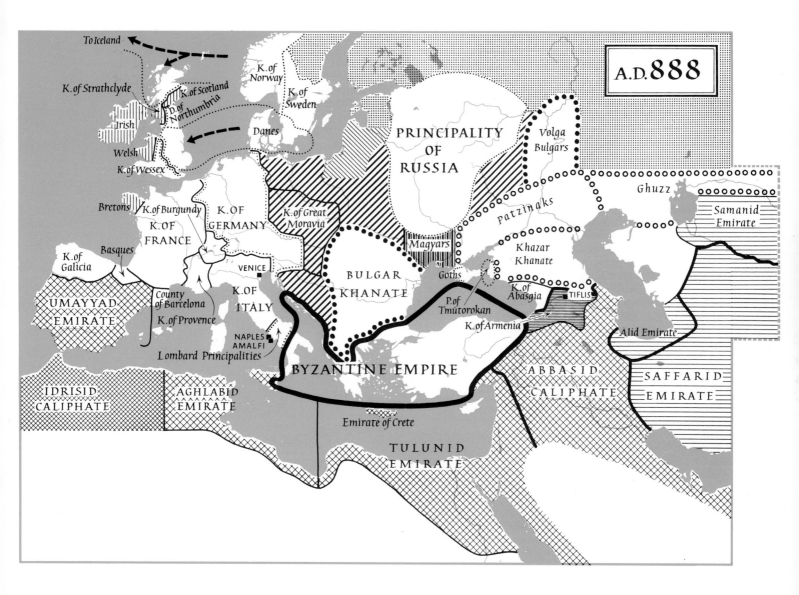

A.D. 888

To Iceland

K. of Strathclyde

K. of Scotland
D. of Northumbria
Irish

Welsh

K. of Wessex

Bretons

K. of Burgundy
Basques
K. of Galicia

K. OF FRANCE

County of Barcelona
K. of Provence

UMAYYAD EMIRATE

IDRISID CALIPHATE

AGHLABID EMIRATE

Emirate of Crete

K. of Norway

K. of Sweden

Danes

K. OF GERMANY

K. of Great Moravia

VENICE

K. OF ITALY

NAPLES
AMALFI
Lombard Principalities

PRINCIPALITY OF RUSSIA

Volga Bulgars

Patzinaks

Magyars

Ghuzz

Samanid Emirate

BULGAR KHANATE

Goths

Khazar Khanate

P. of Tmutorokan

K. of Abasgia

TIFLIS

K. of Armenia

Alid Emirate

BYZANTINE EMPIRE

TULUNID EMIRATE

ABBASID CALIPHATE

SAFFARID EMIRATE

923

The Viking and Moslem marauders had already been active for a century when the Magyars arrived in Europe, but it was only then that the misery of Christendom became complete. Forced out of Russia by the Patzinaks (893), the Magyars occupied Hungary (only lightly held by the Bulgars, whose power lay south of the Danube) and with the short-sighted encouragement of the German King spent the opening years of the tenth century destroying the Empire of Great Moravia. Then their horsemen turned to raiding that was as rapid, widespread, and savage as that of the sea-borne pirates. The unhappy condition of the West at the time is well shown in the history of Burgundy, a state which would appear to be comparatively inaccessible, but which within half a century was raped by Viking, Moslem, and Magyar in turn.

Towards the end of this period the Viking contribution was lessening; the Danes in England were forced to recognize the supremacy of Wessex (918). But the Norse, whose efforts were less dispersed and whose opponents were less organized, not only maintained their hold on Scotland but conquered the southern seaboard of Ireland (914) and revived the Viking grip on the north of England (920). The only achievement of the Danes was the colonization of Normandy, ceded by the French King (911), who was busy expanding his frontiers at the expense of an ailing Germany.

On the other hand, the Moslem raiding grew more severe. Corsica and Sardinia were abandoned by Christendom, though since they were not effectively occupied by the Moslems their status is as uncertain as their actual state was wretched. The Umayyad pirates, using Fraxinetum in Provence as a permanent base, penetrated the mainland of Europe further than ever before; the Fatimids, a Shiite dynasty who replaced the Aghlabids in Tunisia (909), maintained the maritime interests of their predecessors. The demise of the Aghlabids meant the end of even nominal Abbasid control in Tunisia, but elsewhere the Abbasid power underwent a minor revival bringing Egypt under its direct rule (905) and profiting in the east from the overthrow of the pro-Shiite Saffarids by the orthodox and formally obedient Samanids (900). But the revolt of the Qarmatians (899), a Shiite sect that dominated Arabia, was a severe blow to Abbasid prestige, and the independent manners of the Sajid Emir of Azerbaijan marked the continuance of the old centrifugal tendencies. The activities of the Sajid Emir were mostly directed towards depriving the Armenians of their already small store of wealth and happiness; his subtlest approach to the problem was the creation of a rival Armenian Kingdom (Vaspurakan, 908); the bitter rivalry between the new and the original foundations enabled Armenians too to taste the delights of massacring Armenians.

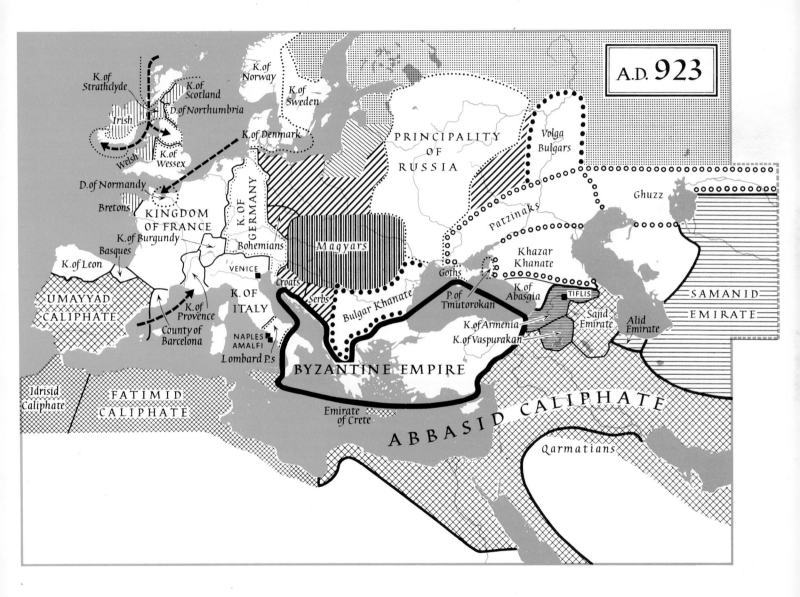

A.D. **923**

K.of Strathclyde
K.of Scotland
Irish
D.of Northumbria
Welsh
K.of Wessex
D.of Normandy
Bretons
KINGDOM OF FRANCE
K.of Burgundy
Basques
K.of Leon
UMAYYAD CALIPHATE
K.of Provence
County of Barcelona
K.of Denmark
K.of Norway
K.of Sweden
K.OF GERMANY
Bohemians
VENICE
K.OF ITALY
NAPLES
AMALFI
Lombard P.s
Croats
Serbs
Magyars
Bulgar Khanate
BYZANTINE EMPIRE
Emirate of Crete
Idrisid Caliphate
FATIMID CALIPHATE
PRINCIPALITY OF RUSSIA
Volga Bulgars
Patzinaks
Goths
Khazar Khanate
P. of Tmutorokan
K.of Abasgia
TIFLIS
K.of Armenia
K.of Vaspurakan
Sajid Emirate
Alid Emirate
Ghuzz
SAMANID EMIRATE
ABBASID CALIPHATE
Qarmatians

998

In the early part of the tenth century even the most stolid would have had adequate reason for heeding the gloomy predictions of pious numerologists concerning the approaching millennium, but in fact the state of Christendom improved considerably as A.D.1000 came nearer. The Magyar, Moslem, and Viking scourges lost their bite, though only the Magyars were brought to a definite stop. The Moslem raids were diminished by the extirpation of Fraxinetum (975), the rise of the Italian seaports, and the revival of Byzantine sea-power. The Vikings, overcome in England and Ireland, retained only Greenland, Iceland,[1] Orkney, and Normandy, of which Normandy alone was expanding and, as the rewards of piracy diminished, their raids died away.

The decisive defeat of the Magyars at the Lechfeld (955), which began the transformation of an Asiatic horde into the Christian Kingdom of Hungary, was inflicted on them by the resurgent Germans. Under the Saxon dynasty the German Kingdom regained (925) the territory previously lost to France, defeated the Danes, and by bringing Bohemia, Moravia, and the Elbe–Oder Slavs into dependence, began the process of Germanization that (in the Elbe–Oder region) took two hundred years to complete and was never to have more than superficial success in Bohemia and Moravia. The annexation of north Italy (951–61) converted the Kingdom into an Empire; the payment by the embryonic Polish Principality of a homage that it was beyond the power of the Empire to extract encouraged the view that a Roman peace had been recreated by the German nation. But the Empire that had been resurrected was Charlemagne's, not Constantine's; it suffered from the same deficiencies in its lack of bureaucracy and its extreme dependence on the personality of its ruler. Moreover, although possessing a

52

much smaller slice of Western Christendom, its pretensions were much greater and the Imperial title soon became its severest handicap.

In the same period the slow shrinkage of the Byzantine Empire was reversed; the reconquest of Crete (961) and Cyprus (965) more than compensated for the loss of the last of Sicily (965), and advances were made on land. But gains at the expense of the fragmented Lombard and Armenian Principalities and the annexation of minor and unsupported Emirates emphasized not so much the health of the Empire, though that had obviously improved, as the sickness of its enemies. Similarly it was a Russian invasion that broke the power of the Bulgarian Empire and enabled the Byzantines to reduce its eastern half (972). The Varangian Principality of Russia reached its peak in the 960s, when it included the whole of south Russia between Don and Danube. Prince Sviatoslav pillaged both Khazars and Bulgars, but his death (972) in a Patzinak ambush was ignominious, and his acquisitions proved impermanent.[2]

The dominion of the Abbasid Caliphate,[3] though not the Caliphate itself, was extinguished by the Buwayhids, a pro-Shiite Persian dynasty to whom the Emirs of Mesopotamia and western Persia paid a general homage that gives a false impression of Buwayhid strength, an impression emphasized by the rapid decline of their main rivals, the Samanids, who were deprived of Transoxiana by the Karakhanid Turks (990). In fact, the maintenance of their largely illusory power was the limit of Buwayhid capabilities.

Another Caliphate to disappear was that of the Moroccan Idrisids, who disintegrated under Fatimid and Umayyad attacks. When the Fatimids conquered Egypt (967–72) their interest in Morocco declined, and it was the Umayyads who obtained its submission. The now largely Berber armies of the Spanish Caliphate[4] also periodically

devastated the Christian Kingdoms of the north, but, though the Moslem supremacy in Spain had never before been so strikingly enforced, the victories were not followed up. The Christian kings paid their tribute and survived their defeats.

The original Georgian Kingdoms had not reappeared on the Arab withdrawal from Transcaucasia. The Lazicans had early been 'liberated' by their kinsmen the Abasgians; the Iberians had accepted the rule of Armenian princes. When Abasgia rechristened herself Georgia (978) she was making a bid for the support of a pan-Georgian patriotism that was then beginning to make itself apparent.

---

1. Iceland was colonized c. 885, Greenland c. 990. Neither they nor the Orkneys were significantly populated before the Norse colonization.

2. The absorption by the Slavs of their Scandinavian overlords is adequately attested in the name Sviatoslav, and the Principality of Russia is therefore no longer marked as Scandinavian. The dichotomy between Russians and other Slavs, increasingly apparent from this time on, justifies the introduction of a new shading at this point.

3. The Caliphate, its temporal claims very much in abeyance, thus comes to an approximate correspondance with the Papacy.

4. The title of Caliph was taken by the Umayyads of Spain in 929.

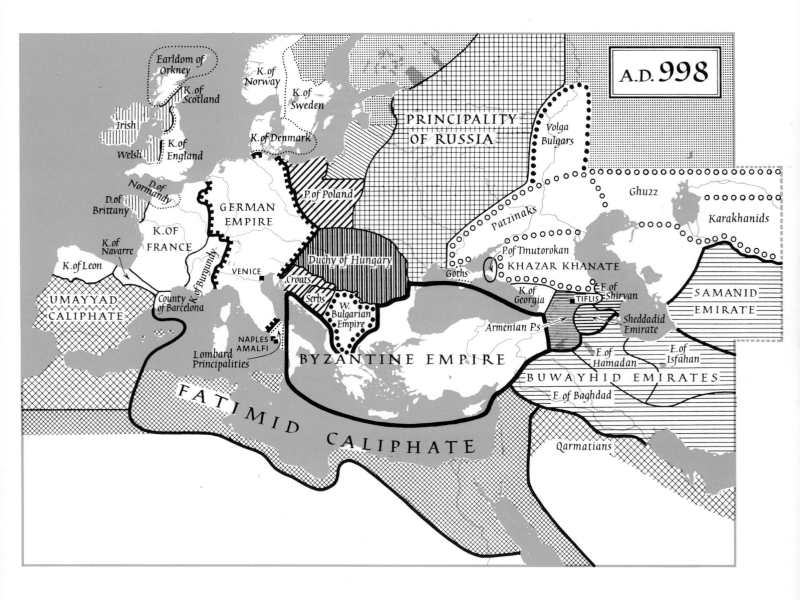

A.D. 998

Earldom of Orkney

K. of Norway

K. of Scotland

Irish

Welsh

K. of England

D. of Normandy

D. of Brittany

K. of Navarre

K. of Leon

UMAYYAD CALIPHATE

County of Barcelona

K. OF FRANCE

K. of Burgundy

GERMAN EMPIRE

K. of Sweden

K. of Denmark

P. of Poland

VENICE

Croats

Serbs

Duchy of Hungary

W. Bulgarian Empire

Lombard Principalities

NAPLES
AMALFI

BYZANTINE EMPIRE

PRINCIPALITY OF RUSSIA

Volga Bulgars

Patzinaks

Goths

P. of Tmutorokan

KHAZAR KHANATE

K. of Georgia

Armenian Ps.

TIFLIS

E. of Shirvan

Sheddadid Emirate

Ghuzz

Karakhanids

SAMANID EMIRATE

E. of Hamadan

E. of Isfahan

BUWAYHID EMIRATES

E. of Baghdad

Qarmatians

FATIMID CALIPHATE

1028

From the peak of success, the Umayyad Caliphate of Spain rapidly descended into oblivion. Civil war between Arabs and Berbers became endemic, and though the Caliphate lingered on till 1031 it was as an impotent spectator. Berber Emirs proclaimed their independence in the south and west of Spain and in Morocco; the eastern seaports soon followed. The Christian states tentatively renewed their attacks, particularly the Basques of Navarre, who had been largely insulated from the ravages visited on their neighbours in previous decades by the ruggedness of their scenery. The mountain Kingdom's most important gain, however, was the province of Castile (1026), was made at the expense of the fellow Christian Kingdom of Leon.

It was not only in Europe that Islam was in decay; the Fatimids[1] and Buwayhids might continue in the appearance of strength, but there was little vigour in either. In striking contrast to dynasties alternately factitious and inert is the Ghaznavid Emirate, founded by a Turkish general (Turks had been the staple of the Near-Eastern Moslem army for more than a century) who overthrew his Samanid master in 999 and seized the vacant throne. The aggression of the Ghaznavids emphasized the bankruptcy of the older foundations, but though they were soon pressing the Buwayhids their conquests are part of Indian, rather than of Near-Eastern history. During this period the Byzantines eliminated the west-Bulgarian Empire (1018) and reduced the Serbs[2] to vassalage; conquered the Crimea (1016); and annexed the Armenian Kingdom of Vaspurakan (1022), no mean list of achievements for a state whose arteries were a great deal harder than those of its Islamic rivals.

Although the Viking epoch had ended with the creation and Christianization of the Scandinavian kingdoms, Denmark at least still cherished the old ambitions, and these were gloriously if briefly fulfilled under Canute. By his adroit government, Canute made England, the superficial conquest of his father (1012), the contented province of an Empire whose resources were insufficient to hold it by force. He was unable to do the same for Norway; her submission (1028) was bitter and temporary. Another small nation, Poland, piled up a dangerous amount of glory at this time. The Principality was enlarged at the expense of Germany, Hungary, and Russia.[3] A policy of all round aggression, however much it may influence people, wins few friends and these successes cast a shadow across the future of a state fundamentally weaker than any of its neighbours. The prudent Scots were wiser when they took a small, digestible slice of England (1018), a gain that strengthened the Kingdom without increasing its commitments.

1. The secession of the Fatimids' Western Provinces was not an important loss, for their Zirid governors had been largely autonomous since the Fatimid removal to Egypt.

2. The southernmost of the two groups (Croats and Serbs) into which the south Slavs had separated.

3. Russia plunged into civil war on the death of St Vladimir (1015) and peace was only achieved (1024) by the division of the country between the Princes of Novgorod and Chernigov – the latter also holding Tmutorokan – while the backwater of Polotsk was left in independence. Unity was restored (except for Polotsk) when the Prince of Chernigov died (1036), but only lasted eighteen years (to 1054).

54

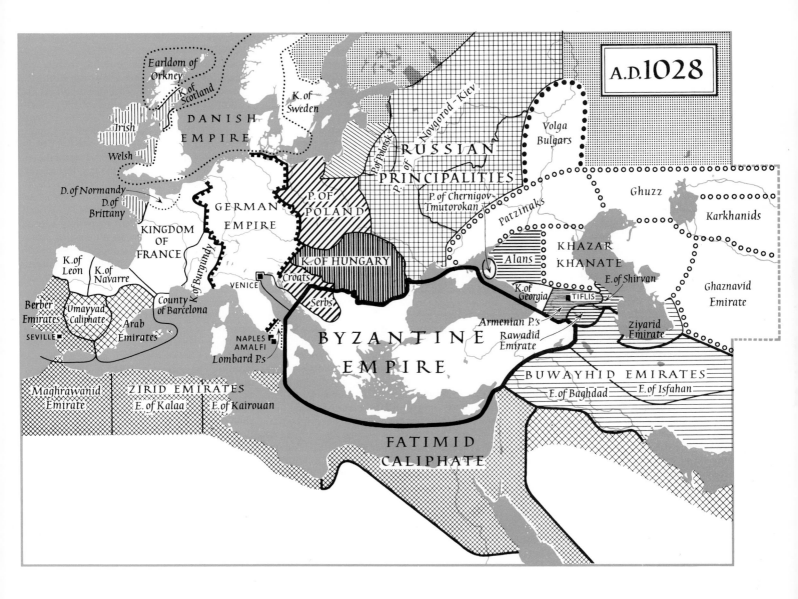

A.D. 1028

Earldom of Orkney
K. of Scotland
Irish
Welsh
DANISH EMPIRE
K. of Sweden
D. of Normandy
D. of Brittany
KINGDOM OF FRANCE
GERMAN EMPIRE
P. OF POLAND
P. of Polotsk
Novgorod – Kiev
RUSSIAN PRINCIPALITIES
Volga Bulgars
P. of Chernigov-Tmutorokan
Patzinaks
Ghuzz
Karkhanids
K. of Burgundy
K. of Hungary
Croats
Serbs
VENICE
Alans
KHAZAR KHANATE
K. of León
K. of Navarre
County of Barcelona
Berber Emirates
Umayyad Caliphate
SEVILLE
Arab Emirates
NAPLES
AMALFI
Lombard P.s
BYZANTINE EMPIRE
K. of Georgia
TIFLIS
E. of Shirvan
Armenian P.s
Rawadid Emirate
Ziyarid Emirate
Ghaznavid Emirate
BUWAYHID EMIRATES
E. of Baghdad
E. of Isfahan
Maghrawanid Emirate
ZIRID EMIRATES
E. of Kalaa
E. of Kairouan
FATIMID CALIPHATE

1028 R

Although the Lombard threat forced the Pope to surrender the territory of Rome to the Franks, he hoped to keep his freedom of action and, by crowning the Carolingians first Kings and then Emperors, to return the obligation. Charlemagne's views on the Papacy were, however, quite Byzantine, and the Pope, feeling that it would be unwise to provoke trouble, meekly accepted a secondary position until the divisions of the Empire after 830 made it easy to re-establish Papal independence. The Carolingians then found that the Pope, not content to draw level, was moving on ahead. The extreme Papal claims were expressed in a document purporting to be the will of the Emperor Constantine in which he left the temporal rule of the whole West to the Vicar of Christ. The Kings of the West were thus merely tenants of the Pope, and their position had to be ratified by him. The fact that this detail had never been observed was hardly surprising, as Constantine seems to have neglected to draw up his will until he had been dead for four hundred years; but, by seeking the Pope's blessing for their usurpation of the throne of Clovis and by allowing the Pope to proclaim the Frankish Empire of the West, the Carolingians had put themselves in a difficult position. In the uncertain retrospect of the times these actions seemed to the following generation a tacit admission of the Papal suzerainty that had not been mooted when they occurred. Yet the darkness of the Dark Ages was a two-edged sword; if it made possible the acceptance of an obvious forgery, men were too illiterate and life too chaotic for any document to exert much effect. Though, for example, the Papal authority over the Church had never been challenged in the West, with the disintegration of the feeble machinery of Carolingian government there was no means of turning the Papal prestige into actual power; Papal commands to the Church could not be heard above the clang of arms; commands to the temporal authorities seemed, in the circumstances, ludicrous. The independence of the Pope became that of a Roman bishop; soon, the confusion increasing, even that was lost and the Pope became the puppet, not of some great power, that could at least maintain the oecumenical dignity, but of the petty barons of Central Italy. Two hundred years after cutting itself off from the Byzantine world, the Papacy found itself in outer darkness.

Although, with the end of iconoclasm in 843, a formal reconciliation between Byzantium and Rome took place, minor doctrinal differences were soon found to maintain the cleft between the two which fundamentally concerned the relative positions of Church and State. On the rapid decline of the Papacy, the direct quarrel lapsed, but competition was fierce in the missionary field, where both gained considerable success. The first area of conflict was Bohemia, where the original endeavour was Eastern (860) but the final victory Catholic (890). At the same time Bulgaria (870) and Serbia (879) were won for the East and the Croats (879) for the West. Around the year 1000, both Churches enlarged further: the Eastern by the admission of the Russians (988), the Catholic by the conversion of the Poles, Magyars, and Scandinavians. The Slavs of the German border were conquered, rather than converted, as were the Saxons before them, and the revival of Christian Spain was also more a matter of sword than word. The Byzantine advance, unfortunately for them, either absorbed already converted countries or uncovered schismatics such as the Armenian Monophysites.

Asceticism is a component of all religious movements and, though more prominent in the Orient, was always present in Christianity. Emulation of the lonely hermits soon led to the hermit colony and this to the monastery, which institution became wide-spread in the Eastern provinces of the Empire in the fourth century. The Byzantine monasteries were many and powerful, though they were diminished in number and wealth during the iconoclastic controversy, when their opposition to the imperial decrees resulted in a definite persecution. The type of monastery initiated by St Benedict in the West was different from its Eastern models in that it fed and maintained itself by its own endeavour, rather than depending on the endowments of the pious, and though the deteriorating conditions of the ninth and early tenth centuries caused a sharp drop in Benedictine standards the Cluniac reform of the tenth–eleventh centuries raised the Western monastery beyond the previous level. It became an oasis of peace, learning, and stability, irrigating the potentially fertile ground around it. The Cluniacs played an important part in the upswing of prosperity that heralded the opening of Christianity's second millennium.

What discussion of Islam is undertaken in this book will be found scattered through the series of maps as a whole, but it is pertinent to observe here the parallel between Shiitism and the Christian heresies. The provinces of the Caliphate in many cases first seceded in the name of Ali (Spain is an exception, but the Umayyad cause was a sufficient distinction). Their independence soon passed beyond challenge and the second generation of Emirates, the Murabits, Zirids, and Samanids, returned to orthodoxy, readily acknowledging a community of culture with Baghdad, once doing so did not prejudice their freedom.

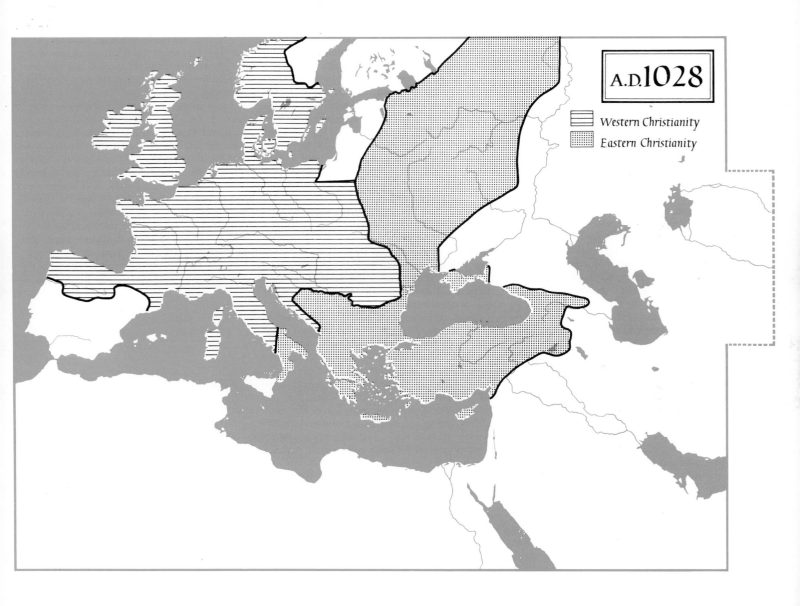

A.D. 1028

Western Christianity
Eastern Christianity

1028 E

The routes of the Vikings and Varangians dominate the northern half of this map. The Vikings expanded the Frisian North Sea traffic in fish, wine, beer, salt, and metals and extended it into the Atlantic. It was probably they who first supplied English wool to the Flemish cloth industry when it began to outrun the supply from France. To the East, the Varangians opened up routes that traversed the whole of Russia and broke the Khazar grip on the trade to Constantinople. As before, the amber, fur, and slave trades provided the basis of business with the Byzantine and Islamic Empires, but wax and honey were also exported. Wax and tallow candles were steadily replacing vegetable-oil lamps, and in this the liturgical needs of religion gave a lead. Honey was a valuable sweetening matter, the only one known in the West, where sugar, an expensive spice, was used as a medicine. Viking–Varangian activity, ranging from Iceland to the borders of Turkestan, from Constantinople to the Arctic circle, was of incredible vitality and daring, and it is sad that so much of the effort was wasted in plundering. The northern heroes did not deign to trade until they had failed to vanquish; they preferred bloodstained, glorious gold to a steady mercantile profit.

It is not possible to show the basic growth that was taking place in the Western economy at this time. The population, the urban in particular, was increasing – hamlets expanding into villages and villages into small towns. Yet the operative word is small, and none of the new towns can qualify for inclusion here. The only exception is Venice, and its rise appears merely to compensate for the fall of Ravenna and the eclipse of Rome. So what cannot be shown must be borne in mind – the final crumbling of the last centres of Roman civilization was accompanied by the appearance of new foci, small but numerous.

Venice owed its rise to its political independence, the gift of its island sites; and to its shrewd acceptance of a formal Byzantine suzerainty under cover of which it was able to monopolize the East–West trade. State legislation enforcing low interest rates for agricultural reasons discouraged the Byzantines from entering such a high-risk business as long-distance trading; the ever-needy exchequer bore heavily on even the humblest merchant. Crushed by the overheads of Empire, the Byzantines could not compete with the Venetians even on internal routes, and a Venetian network began to replace the native Byzantine one. In return for the loan of their fleet, the Venetians secured preferential rates on the taxes they did pay (992), and in 1081 they were able to extort from the collapsing Empire the right to trade anywhere within its boundaries without restriction or taxation of any kind. Carrying such a mortgage, the revived Byzantine Empire of the early twelfth century can only be called a sham.

In 750, knowledge of the Chinese process of manufacturing paper from flax and old linen reached Turkestan. It spread slowly throughout Islam, reached Sicily and Spain in the twelfth century, Italy in the thirteenth, and Germany in the first half of the fourteenth. The export of papyrus by Egypt had ceased around 700; after the introduction of paper manufacture in the tenth century, the making of papyrus stopped entirely. The loss of the useless monopoly did Egypt little harm; in time she became a considerable exporter of paper.

In the early Middle Ages, when transport was costly and uncertain, a local source of raw material, even if a poor one, was worth working. Deposits of iron ore, for example, are widespread in the West, and it was not until transport costs came down that it mattered much that Scandinavia and Germany produced the best and cheapest iron. At the other end of the scale, England had an effective monopoly of tin in the West, and Spain of mercury, simply because no one else had very much at all. Similarly, most western gold came from Bohemia.

Lead, silver, and copper came somewhere in between these two classes: most countries had workable deposits, but from the tenth century Germany and to a lesser extent Scandinavia created and dominated foreign markets. All this ignores the East. There the mines of antiquity were largely worked out, and with the rise in consumption of metal the Byzantine and Islamic countries became importers. Only Armenia and metroplitan Persia produced any considerable amount of ore; for the rest, Byzantium relied on Western Europe, Islam on Western Europe and Turkestan.

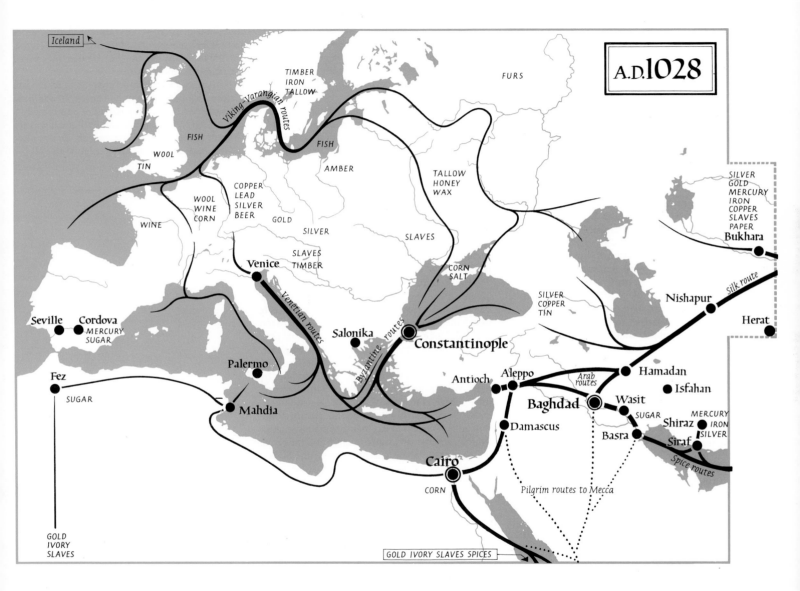

Iceland

A.D.1028

TIMBER
IRON
TALLOW

FURS

Viking-Varangian routes

FISH

FISH

WOOL
TIN

AMBER

TALLOW
HONEY
WAX

SILVER
GOLD
MERCURY
IRON
COPPER
SLAVES
PAPER

Bukhara

COPPER
LEAD
SILVER
BEER

WOOL
WINE
CORN

GOLD

SILVER

SLAVES

CORN
SALT

SILVER
COPPER
TIN

Silk route

Nishapur

WINE

SLAVES
TIMBER

Venice

Herat

Venetian routes

Salonika

Byzantine routes

Constantinople

Hamadan

Isfahan

Seville   Cordova
           MERCURY
           SUGAR

Palermo

Antioch   Aleppo

Arab
routes

Baghdad

Wasit

MERCURY
IRON
SILVER

Shiraz

Fez

SUGAR

Damascus

SUGAR

Basra

Siraf

Mahdia

Spice routes

Cairo

GOLD
IVORY
SLAVES

CORN

Pilgrim routes to Mecca

GOLD IVORY SLAVES SPICES

1071

The Ghaznavid Emirate, the first of the Moslem Turkish Empires, was soon eclipsed by the Empire of the Seljuks, a clan of mercenary Ghuzz who revolted from Ghaznavid employ in 1037. The growth of the new power was phenomenally fast. By 1055 the Ghaznavids had been expelled from Persia and the Buwayhids conquered. As neither the Seljuks' appetite for war nor their rate of advance showed any signs of slackening, both the Byzantines, who were unable to prevent the conquest of Transcaucasia, and the Fatimids, whose Syrian dependencies were invaded, watched their eastern frontiers with growing concern. Repeated raiding of Byzantine Armenia by the Seljuk Sultan[1] Alp Arslan stimulated an Imperial if sluggish response, the Emperor himself marching against the barbarians who had violated the majesty of New Rome. But there were indications (the loss of Italy, the conquest of the Crimea by the Cumans in 1068, and the revolt of Serbia in 1043) that the Byzantine revival had passed its peak.

Elsewhere in Islam – another verse of the old song. The Fatimids, who had accepted the independence of the Zirids with equanimity, reacted sharply to their apostasy (the Zirids declared themselves Orthodox in 1048), but their revenge was at second hand. Numerous Qarmatian Arab tribes who had been subdued at an earlier date by the Fatimids were launched against the Zirid 'heretics' (1050). The migration of these nomads into the hinterland of Algeria and Tunisia was far more destructive to the North-African economy than the earlier Arab conquest; in fact, the country was ruined more effectively than the Zirids, who lingered on in the fortified seaports. Eastward, Morocco was conquered (1056–64) by the Murabits, Saharan Berbers who brought new vitality to North-African Islam. In Spain, the Arab Emirate of Seville broke the Berber hold on the South, but neither Seville nor any other Spanish Emirate could stand against the Christians of the North, for, although Navarre had been divided, the conquest of Leon by Castile (1037) established a Northern Kingdom capable of exacting the homage of the divided Muslims.

The history of the Ghuzz is far from monopolized by the Seljuk clan, for the main, heathen part of the tribe moved into the Russian steppe (1060), pushing the Patzinaks before them and defeating the South Russian princes (1068).[2] Towards the end of the century, the Cumans, as the Ghuzz were called by the Byzantines, destroyed Tmutorokan; their belligerence threatened the prosperity even more than the security of the south-Russian cities.

If in Islam and Russia the eleventh century is dominated by the Ghuzz, in Europe proper this is the century of the Normans. The blend of Viking and Frank in the Duchy produced a race of hybrid vigour, men who in their ambition and valour established a firmer authority over their subjects than had hitherto existed in the West. William the Bastard, Duke of Normandy, was master of northern France and by marriage the heir to England, which had been independent since the death of Canute (1035) and the break-up of his empire. In 1066, William took up this claim with a mailed fist and began the work of shaping England to his ideas. Normans who received no reward from William's conquest found their opportunity in the chronic enmity of Lombard and Byzantine in southern Italy where the progress of the Seljuk from mercenary to monarch is echoed in the career of the Norman, Robert Guiscard, though his piecemeal conquest of Byzantine Italy took him all of twenty years. He then turned against the Lombards[3] and the Moslems of Sicily. Neither William's nor Guiscard's realms loom large on the map, but this belies their importance, for they were, outside Islam and Byzantium, the first states to be effectively organized since the fall of Rome. Enshrined in the mystique of 1066 is the seed of the national, secular state.

For the moment, the old style German Empire restored its peeling facade. Though it was little strengthened by the acquisition of anarchic Burgundy (1032), the humiliation by Poland was revenged, that country contracting to life size after having made enemies of all its neighbours.

---

1. The title of Sultan, corresponding to Emperor or Khan, implies complete sovereignty and advertises the restriction of the jurisdiction of the Caliph to spiritual matters.

2. The principalities into which Russia was divided in 1054 were theoretically ranked in strict order, with the Great Principality of Kiev taking precedence and exerting a degree of overall control which varied with the personality of the incumbent. When he died, the idea was for all the princes to move up one; but as might be expected, though a prince was always willing to inherit, he was rarely keen to relinquish. The system worked at best spasmodically, with a marked tendency for the principalities to become hereditary in one branch of the Royal House.

3. One of the Lombard principalities, Salerno, had already fallen into the hands of another Norman adventurer (1058).

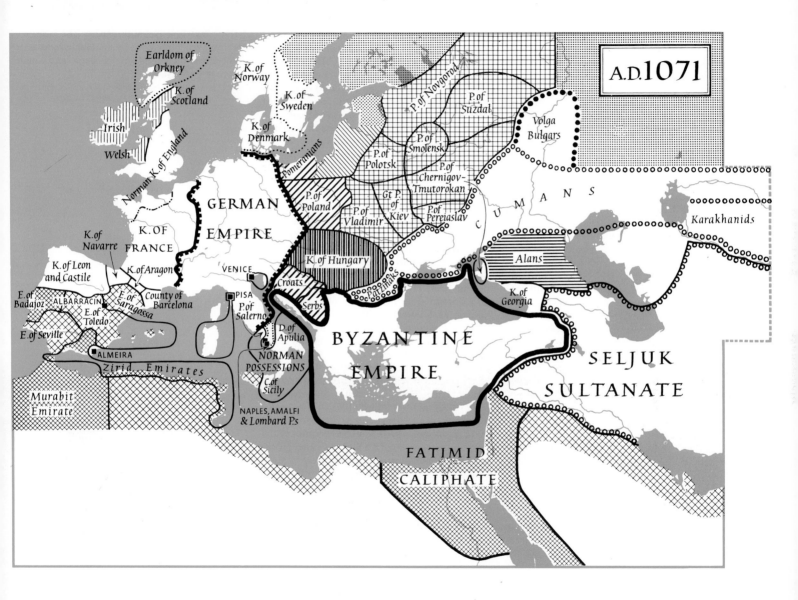

A.D. 1071

Earldom of Orkney

K. of Scotland

Irish

Welsh

K. of England

Norman K. of England

K. of Norway

K. of Sweden

K. of Denmark

Pomeranians

P. of Novgorod

P. of Suzdal

Volga Bulgars

P. of Smolensk

P. of Polotsk

P. of Chernigov-Tmutorokan

GERMAN EMPIRE

P. of Poland

Gt P. of Kiev

P. of Vladimir

P. of Pereiaslav

CUMANS

Karakhanids

K. OF FRANCE

K. of Navarre

K. of Aragon

K. of Leon and Castile

County of Barcelona

E. of Saragossa

ALBARRACIN

E. of Badajoz

E. of Toledo

E. of Seville

ALMEIRA

Zirid Emirates

Murabit Emirate

VENICE

PISA

K. of Hungary

Croats

Serbs

P. of Salerno

D. of Apulia

NORMAN POSSESSIONS

C. of Sicily

NAPLES, AMALFI & Lombard P.s

Pecheneg

Patzinaks

Alans

K. of Georgia

BYZANTINE EMPIRE

SELJUK SULTANATE

FATIMID CALIPHATE

1092

The battle of Manzikert (1071), in which the Byzantine army was destroyed by the Seljuks, is unimpeachably one of the decisive battles of history. Adrianople had been an equally crushing defeat from the strictly military point of view, but it had few consequences for the East. After Manzikert, there was nothing to oppose the Turkish flood, and only the Bosphorus saved the Empire. Alp Arslan himself did not follow up his victory (he was killed shortly after, fighting the Karakhanids, who were absorbed by the Seljuks in 1073), and the conquest of Anatolia was really a migration of Turkish tribes into the vacuum that Manzikert had created. It completely by-passed the Armenians in the uninviting Taurus mountains.[1] The European rump of the Byzantine Empire had its own troubles to cope with, for Patzinak and Cuman raids and an invasion by Guiscard had to be repelled; but by the last years of the eleventh century, Europe was quieter and the decay of the Seljuk sultanate offered the chance of limited reconquest in Asia. However, the Byzantine appeal to the Christian West for mercenaries precipitated the first Crusade, an exaggerated response and, for Eastern Christianity, a threatening one. The Crusaders' blend of cupidity and fanaticism made them dangerous allies; their enthusiasm did not stem from sympathy with the hard-pressed Byzantines whom they regarded with suspicion, but from a desire to free the Holy Places from the Turks whose conversion to Islam was too recent for them to allow Christian pilgrimage as had the tolerant Fatimids.

It was, however, in the Moslem world that fanaticism was carried to its extreme – by the Shiite sect of Assassins, who exerted an influence out of proportion to their number by the unsparing use of the political technique to which they have given their name. This in turn derives from hashish, the effect of which was interpreted as a glimpse of the paradise to come and made the initiates of the sect impatient of this world and oblivious of the personal consequences of their acts. Lodges, secret and open, existed throughout the Middle East, receiving their instructions from the fortress of Alamut in Tabaristan, where the headquarters of the sect were set up in 1090. Assassin activities were limited to the Islamic world and did not affect the Christians.

Besides the catastrophe in the East, the other events in Christendom seem trivial, though the taking of Toledo (1085) was the first great step in the reconquest of Spain. The advance was halted by the Murabits of Morocco, who crossed the Straits of Gibraltar at the request of the Spanish Muslims (1086). By 1092 they had incorporated into their Empire all the Spanish emirates except Badajoz, Albarracin, and Saragossa, which they took in 1094, 1103, and 1110 respectively. On the Christian side, the crowns of Aragon and Navarre were united in 1076.

The Normans continued to expand; the conquest of Sicily was completed and the last Lombard states were annexed by their south-Italian group; in the North the separation of the Duchy from England on William's death caused it to lose ground, though England gained territory from the Scots (1092) and the Welsh (1093). (The Anglo-Scottish border now takes on its final form, while the not-quite-completed Scottish conquest of the mainland possessions of the Earl of Orkney (1078) begins the elimination of the Norse element from Scottish history.) The growing power of the Papacy and its fatally disruptive quarrel with the German Emperor which began at this time are covered in a later page, as are the commercial empires of the Italian seaports, whose foundations were laid by the Pisan occupation of Sardinia (1050) and Corsica (1077), and the Venetian of Istria (1000) and Dalmatia (1076). The latter acquisition was threatened by the Hungarians after 1097, when they conquered Croatia, and finally lost to them in 1108.

1. The Armenian princes expropriated by the Byzantines had been given estates in this region, and when the Turkish raids began in the 1050s large numbers of Armenians travelled to these safer lands, so that although Armenia proper does not appear again in this series, lesser Armenia, in the Taurus, remains for a while yet.

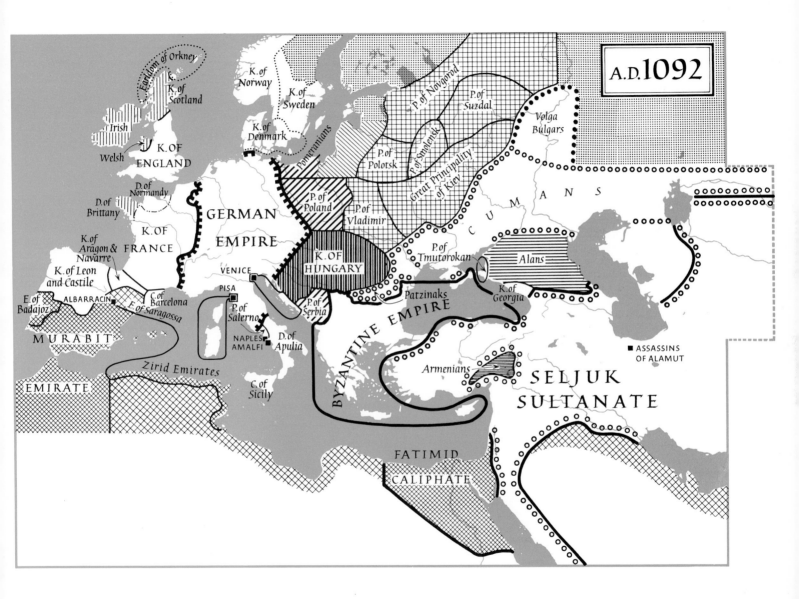

A.D. 1092

Earldom of Orkney

K. of Norway

K. of Scotland

K. of Sweden

Irish

Welsh

K. OF ENGLAND

K. of Denmark

Pomeranians

P. of Novgorod

P. of Suzdal

Volga Bulgars

D. of Normandy

GERMAN EMPIRE

P. of Poland

P. of Vladimir

P. of Polotsk

P. of Smolensk

Great Principality of Kiev

D. of Brittany

K. OF FRANCE

K. OF HUNGARY

CUMANS

K. of Aragon & Navarre

VENICE

P. of Tmutorokan

Alans

K. of Leon and Castile

PISA

P. of Salerno

P. of Serbia

Patzinaks

K. of Georgia

E. of Badajoz

ALBARRACIN

C. of Barcelona

E. of Saragossa

NAPLES AMALFI

D. of Apulia

BYZANTINE EMPIRE

Armenians

MURABIT

Zirid Emirates

C. of Sicily

SELJUK SULTANATE

■ ASSASSINS OF ALAMUT

EMIRATE

FATIMID CALIPHATE

1130

The first Crusade was a great success, but it left the Near East deplorably congested with petty states. Both the success and the congestion were largely due to the breakdown of the central Seljuk power; for of the sultanates of Nicaea, Hamadan, and Merv into which the Empire split, only Merv, the easternmost, retained a measure of power and stability. The sultanate of Nicaea, which inherited the lands conquered from the Byzantines, was unable to extract obedience from its dependants, the Danishmandids, who held nearly half their territory, and its power was temporarily broken by the defeat it suffered at the hands of the Crusaders when they debouched from Constantinople in 1097. The Crusaders marched straight through to Antioch, but the Byzantines held on to some of the ground, including Nicaea, that had been cleared of Turks in the process, while subsidiary Imperial campaigns regained the Black Sea and Mediterranean coasts. The Danishmandid Emirate was comparatively strengthened and became quite oblivious of Seljuk authority, now recentred on Iconium.

The western marches of the Sultanate of Hamadan were in the hands of numerous independent emirs,[1] who unaided were unable to prevent the foundation of the crusading states of Antioch, Tripoli, Edessa, and Jerusalem (1097–9), and when the Georgians swept from obscurity into Tiflis (1121) the Christian advance reached threatening proportions. It was Zangi, Emir of Mosul, who brought it to a halt and began the counter-attack. As well as reaping some of the profits of the first Crusade, the Byzantines brought the Serbs to heel and destroyed the Patzinaks (1122), while the defeat of the Cumans by the Russian principality, now reunified for the last time (1113–32), relieved the Empire of their raids. Once again, Byzantium had survived the apparently ultimate *débâcle*.

The conquests of the Normans in Southern Italy were consolidated by Roger of Sicily, who brought the kingdom he created (1129) to the zenith of its power when he annexed the Zirid emirates of Tunisia (1134–53).[2] In wealth and civilization, his court rivalled that of Constantinople. Normandy itself, pawned by its Duke to raise money for the first Crusade, passed to his fraternal creditor, the King of England, when the Duke on his return proved incapable of redeeming it.

For the rest, Poland subdued the Pomeranians (1102–24), Norway the Orkneys (1098), both enforcing the homage they claimed the right to expect. The counties of Barcelona and Provence were united in 1112. Aragon and Navarre separated in 1134, but whereas Aragon advanced its small frontier aggressively, Navarre became a backwater and soon (1200) lost half its territory to Castile.

1. Many were actually entitled 'atabegs' (guardians), as they governed on behalf of infant Seljuk princes, but their inability to keep their charges alive soon outpaced the fertility of the Seljuk house. The atabegs are incomparable material for the professional rehabilitators, but, until such time as the partisans of Richard III are free to take up this challenge, it would seem safer to use the non-commital title of emir.

2. Naples was taken in 1150 and the northern frontier advanced slightly in 1144.

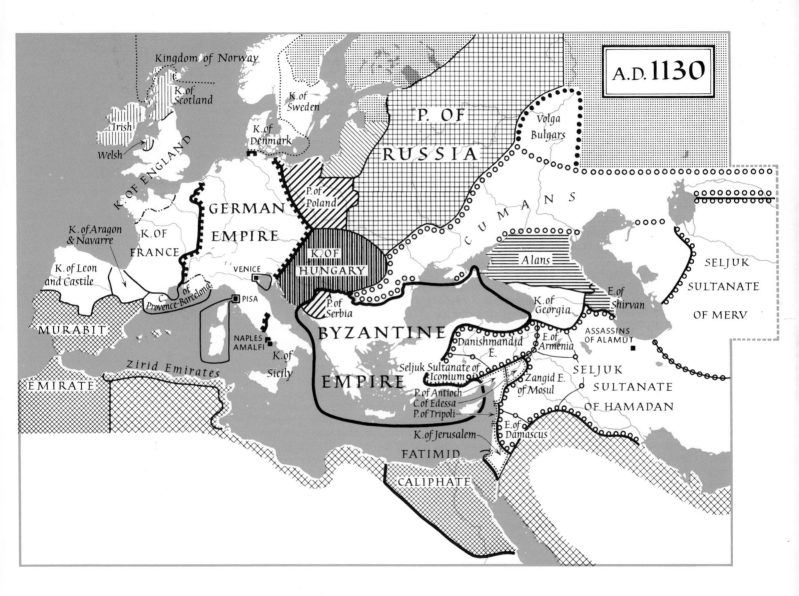

A.D. 1130

Kingdom of Norway

K. of Scotland

Irish

Welsh

K.of Sweden

K. of Denmark

P. OF RUSSIA

Volga Bulgars

K. OF ENGLAND

GERMAN EMPIRE

P. of Poland

K. OF FRANCE

K. of Aragon & Navarre

K. of Leon and Castile

C. of Provence-Barcelona

VENICE

PISA

K. OF HUNGARY

P. of Serbia

CUMANS

Alans

K. of Georgia

E. of Shirvan

SELJUK SULTANATE OF MERV

MURABIT

NAPLES AMALFI

K. of Sicily

Zirid Emirates

BYZANTINE

EMPIRE

Danishmandid E.

Seljuk Sultanate of Iconium

P. of Antioch

C. of Edessa

P. of Tripoli

K. of Jerusalem

E. of Armenia

ASSASSINS OF ALAMUT

Zangid E. of Mosul

SELJUK SULTANATE OF HAMADAN

EMIRATE

FATIMID

CALIPHATE

E. of Damascus

1173

The fall of the sultanate of Merv, the only powerful Seljuk state, echoes the birth of the dynasty; it crumbled into anarchy on the revolt of its Ghuzz mercenaries (1153).[1] The symmetry of Seljuk history is, alas, destroyed by the persistence of the diminished sultanate of Hamadan, in control of no more than its royal domain, and the even more diminished sultanate of Iconium. But though the local rulers who had been under the authority of the Sultan of Hamadan had no difficulty in establishing their independence (the Abbasid Caliph is in this category), the Sultan of Iconium was only prevented from absorbing the Danishmandid and other minor Emirates of Anatolia by unceasing exertion and subsidy on the part of both Byzantines and Zangids, an augur that Seljuk energies were not yet exhausted.

Events in the crusading states are bound up with the expansion of the Zangids. Before his death, Zangi had taken Edessa (1145), and his son Nureddin easily rode out the pitiful second Crusade which was the Christian response. Its failure and the general ill success of later Crusades followed the assumption of Crusading leadership by the Kings of Europe, who could spend but little time in the East and were no substitute for the land-hungry, nothing-to-lose baronage of the first Crusade. In 1154, Moslem Syria was unified by Nureddin's absorption of the Emirate of Damascus and the struggle then moved to Egypt, fat with wealth and convulsed by the death throes of the Fatimid Caliphate. Each side realized the importance of this country, whose resources would decide the outcome of the struggle between Cross and Crescent in the Levant, but the Christians could not prevent victory and Egypt going to Nureddin (1169).

As the Fatimid Caliphate fell to the orthodox Zangids, a Shiite Empire was created further west by the Muwahids, who took over the territories of the dissolving Murabits (1145), expelled the Normans and the remains of the Zirids (1152–60), and enforced their supremacy over the Berber and Arab nomads. The renewed Christian advance in Spain was checked, while the secession of Portugal (1139) and Leon (1157) from Castile dispersed the strength of the northern Kingdom. The union of Aragon and Barcelona (1140) balanced this division, and although the Muwahid Caliphate was of impressive extent the preponderance in Spain had by now passed to the Christians.

The Russian principality was finally split up in 1139, and the vague supremacy that was vested in the Great Princes of Kiev did not survive Kiev's sack at the hands of the Prince of Suzdal (1169). What national authority remained after this devolved on this Prince, who built a new capital (Vladimir in Suzdal, not to be confused with Vladimir in Volhynia) to house his new dignity.[2] In 1138, Poland divided into similarly bickering principalities.

On the extinction of the Norman line in England (1135), the throne passed to the Count of Anjou, who had married the heiress of Aquitaine. The King of England thus held the Norman, Angevin, and Aquitainian fiefs, making him even in France far more powerful than the French King. The English invasion of Ireland (1169), the Swedish settlement of Finland, and the Byzantine conquest of Dalmatia and Croatia are other points to notice. At the other end of the Empire, the Byzantines succeeded in extracting homage from the principality of Antioch, legally due to them, as the Crusaders had agreed to hold in vassalage to the Empire any land they might conquer that lay within the pre-Manzikert Imperial frontier.

1. Before that (1141), Transoxiana had fallen to the Karakhitai, Bhuddist Mongolians, whose Khanate stretched over the whole of Turkestan. This is, incidentally, the only time that a Bhuddist state appears on the map.

2. In most of the Russian principalities a measure of power was held by the merchants of the capital, but in Novgorod the power they wielded was so great that Prince was but the title of their first magistrate and the constitution was in fact republican. As with the Italian and German cities, however, it must be remembered that republican means oligarchic, not democratic, only men of substance having a voice in affairs.

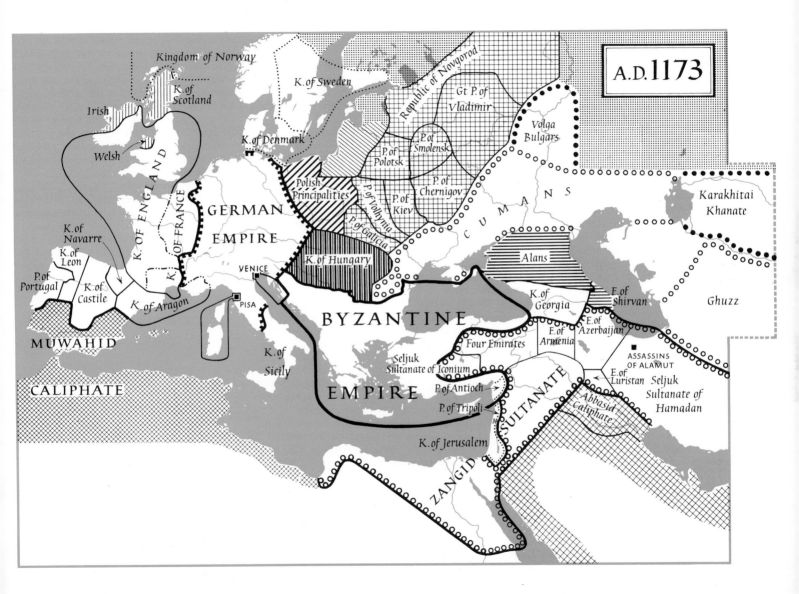

A.D. 1173

Kingdom of Norway

K. of Sweden

Republic of Novgorod

Gt P. of Vladimir

K. of Scotland

Irish

Welsh

K. of Denmark

Volga Bulgars

P. of Smolensk

P. of Polotsk

P. of Chernigov

Karakhitai Khanate

GERMAN EMPIRE

Polish Principalities

P. of Volhynia

P. of Kiev

CUMANS

K. OF ENGLAND

K. OF FRANCE

K. of Navarre

K. of Leon

P. of Portugal

K. of Castile

K. OF BURGUNDY

K. of Aragon

VENICE

PISA

K. of Hungary

P. of Galicia

BYZANTINE

Alans

K. of Georgia

E. of Shirvan

Ghuzz

E. of Armenia

E. of Azerbaijan

MUWAHID

CALIPHATE

K. of Sicily

EMPIRE

Seljuk Sultanate of Iconium

Four Emirates

ASSASSINS OF ALAMUT

E. of Luristan

Seljuk Sultanate of Hamadan

P. of Antioch

P. of Tripoli

Abbasid Caliphate

K. of Jerusalem

ZANGID SULTANATE

1212

Nureddin continued to reside at Mosul even after the conquest of Egypt, which was ruled in his name by a Kurdish general, Saladin. This was a mistake, for the new tail was capable of wagging the dog, and indeed after Nureddin's death (1174) Saladin set up on his own, the Zangids soon becoming the subordinates of the Ayyubid dynasty that Saladin founded. The success of the new Egyptian sultanate was assured by the victory of Hattin, which reduced the 'Kingdom of Jerusalem' to the single town of Tyre (1187), and although Acre (1191) and a strip of the Palestinian coast were regained by the workmanlike third Crusade, the Kingdom of Acre and the reduced, amalgamated principalities of Antioch and Tripoli were no more than slight blemishes on the face of Saladin's Empire. The third Crusade's biggest success was the seizure of Cyprus (1190) from the weakening Byzantines. The superiority of the Christians at sea made island kingdoms in the East a good proposition.

With the Turks at Iconium, Byzantium could never rest secure. A determined effort was made to dislodge them, but the battle of Myriocephalum (1176) was another Manzikert, and although not exploited by the Turks it left the Empire defenceless. As the paralysed Byzantines waited for catastrophe, the distal provinces of the Empire fell away: Croatia and Dalmatia to Hungary (1188) and south-west Anatolia to the Seljuks (1207), while Serbia, Bulgaria, and Lesser Armenia regained their independence. Yet the Empire existed in a state of stagnant anti-climax for another quarter century, and when the expected end came it was as a stab in the back from the fourth Crusade (1204). The villains of this piece were not the ignorant Crusaders, who blindly cut out the heart of the dying Empire, but the Venetians, whose sly manipulations contrived the final perversion of the enterprise. Having begun by making the Crusaders pay for their passage by taking for Venice the Dalmatian town of Zara (1202), they ended by seizing all the islands that lay on the trade routes they now monopolized. Eight centuries later the fourth Crusade probably retains its place as the greatest commercial *coup* of all time.

Though the Crusaders could destroy the Empire, they could not hold more than a part of it, and four fragments remained under Greek rule.[1] The Despotate of Rhodes was insignificant; the Empire of Trebizond well nourished by trade but dominated politically by the Kingdom of Georgia, now at the height of its power. It was in the Empire of Nicaea and the Despotate of Epirus that hopes for the re-establishment of Byzantine rule in Constantinople were vested.

If the Kingdoms of England and Sicily were no longer in Norman hands (the Kingdom of Sicily had been inherited by the German dynasty of Hohenstaufen in 1194), their machinery remained intact. France, where the monarch had been no more than the chairman of an unruly board of barons, joined the ranks of modern states when the conquest of the English fiefs in France (1205) was clinched by the victory of Bouvines (1214), actually won, it is heartening to learn, over the German allies of the English. The ex-English possessions became the personal property of the French King, making him powerful enough to enforce his supremacy throughout the country.

In contrast, the German Emperors, who had originally held considerable real power, had by this time dissipated it. The extravagance of their pretensions, the uncertain succession, and the quarrel with the Papacy were largely responsible for this. Germany became a loose federation of magnates, to whom the Emperor failed to give a lead on those frontiers where the Empire was still expanding. After half a century's struggle, north Italy successfully repudiated all control, and became a mosaic of city-states that only a legal fiction kept within the Empire. The struggle with Denmark for the Baltic littoral (at this time going in Denmark's favour) was in the hands of purely local forces, as was the eastward drive. This was picking up speed again; west Pomerania was annexed in 1181, and the Knights of the Sword (a permanent organization of Crusaders on the lines of the Templar and other orders evolved in the East) took Riga in 1201.

The recrudescence of one Seljuk sultanate did not save the other from destruction (1194) by the Shah (Sultan) of Khwarizm who created a new Turkish Empire when he chased his Karakhitai overlord out of Transoxiana (1210). The fiefs acquired by Aragon in the south of France at this time did not balance the loss of Provence; indeed they brought only trouble, for they involved her in the Albigensian crusade.

---

1. Five, if we count the fortress of Monemvasia in the Peloponnesus, which held out until 1246.

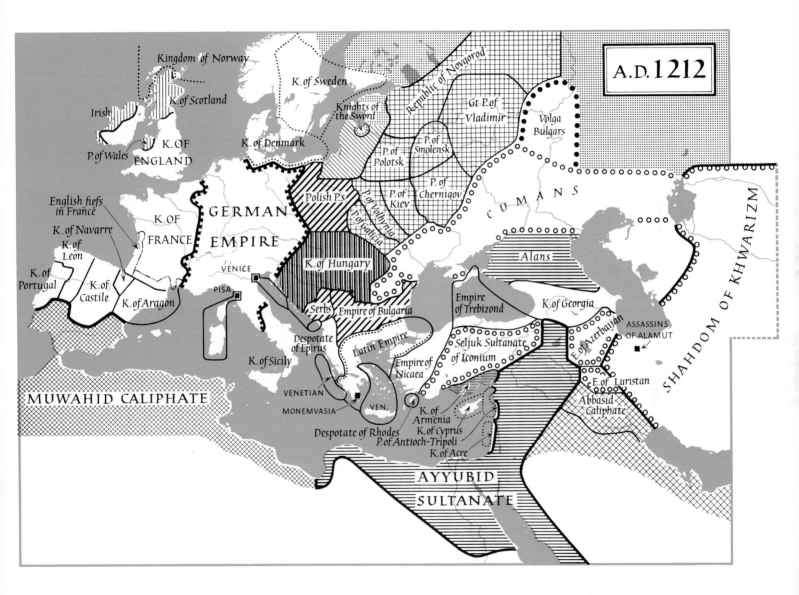

A.D. 1212

Kingdom of Norway

K. of Sweden

Republic of Novgorod

Knights of the Sword

Gt P.of Vladimir

Volga Bulgars

Irish

K. of Scotland

K. OF ENGLAND

P. of Wales

K. of Denmark

P. of Polotsk

P. of Smolensk

P. of Chernigov

English fiefs in France

GERMAN EMPIRE

Polish P.s

P.of Volhynia

P. of Kiev

CUMANS

K. of Navarre

K. of Leon

K. OF FRANCE

P. of Galicia

K. of Portugal

K. of Castile

K. of Aragon

VENICE

K. of Hungary

Alans

PISA

Serbs

Empire of Bulgaria

Empire of Trebizond

K. of Georgia

SHAHDOM OF KHWARIZM

Despotate of Epirus

Latin Empire

Empire of Nicaea

Seljuk Sultanate of Iconium

E. of Azerbaijan

ASSASSINS OF ALAMUT

K. of Sicily

MUWAHID CALIPHATE

VENETIAN

MONEMVASIA

VEN.

Despotate of Rhodes

K. of Armenia

K. of Cyprus

P.of Antioch-Tripoli

K. of Acre

E. of Luristan

Abbasid Caliphate

AYYUBID SULTANATE

1212 R

The history of the Carolingian Empire was a lesson in the impermanence of barbaric success that was not lost on the German Emperors. One way in which they tried to insure against a like fate was by encouraging the reform of the German Church, for the utility of such a movement had been demonstrated by the Cluniacs. Soon the German Emperor and his bishops were cooperating in raising the nation from savagery, rekindling the piety of the brutalized clerics, encouraging their partial literacy and deploring their frequent incontinence. Respect for peace grew with the success of this repair, and the bishops became pillars of the new order; finally (1045), the Emperor salvaged the Papacy and saw that the office was competently filled.

With the memory of its own humiliation still fresh, the Papacy too was determined to prevent a second collapse. Previously, the Papal headship of the Western Church had been passive – the Papacy had been the ultimate court of appeal for ecclesiastics, but had made no move unless appealed to (Gregory the Great (590–604) is the classic exception to this rule). Now Rome actively interfered in provincial affairs, extending its authority through the ramifications of the Church. The first phase of this incredibly rapid rejuvenation ended when the Roman laity was excluded from Papal elections, a move which was more than an attempt to place the Papacy out of reach of the turbulent local nobility. By limiting the right to vote to the Cardinals, it denied the Emperor any part in the election and proclaimed the independence of Pope from State. This revolt went unchallenged – the Emperor Henry IV was a minor and the Regency weak. Lack of opposition encouraged the Papacy to re-publicize the donation of Constantine and revive its extreme doctrine of Pope above State, thus claiming the Empire itself and making conflict inevitable. The Papacy had one advantage to offset its obvious weaknesses: the dependence of the Empire on the German Church, which provided much of the machinery of government. If the Emperor were deprived of any say in the appointment of bishops and if their allegiance could be won by the Papacy, the secular power would wither and be merely the ornament of a theocracy, with ecclesiastics immune from secular obligation.

Papal imperialism was denounced by Henry IV when he obtained power. The first round of the contest ended in a resounding Papal victory, the Emperor doing public penance (1077). But the Papal threat to depose the Emperor would have had little effect had there not already been a powerful revolt in Germany, and once this had been crushed Henry retracted his concessions, declared the Pope deposed in his turn, and carried his own candidate to Rome by force of arms. The Pope fled to the Normans (necessarily opposed to any expansion of Imperial power in Italy), and raised up another Emperor from among the discontented German barons. The struggle fluctuated for half a century, for the Imperial army was too often needed elsewhere for it to garrison Rome permanently, and, once it left, the real Pope returned. Most men acknowledged the Emperor but not his puppet Pope, and the Pope but not his puppet Emperor. In 1122 came the compromise: Pope and Emperor, frightened by the growing lawlessness the continual civil war engendered, agreed to abandon their puppets and the joint appointment of bishops. Peace was uneasy and, in the long struggle for independence of the north-Italian towns, the Pope proved a willing ally against the Emperor, for, though the disintegration of the Empire would expose the Papacy to harsher winds, few Popes could resist rocking its creaking structure.

At the start of the thirteenth century papal power reached its peak. The German Empire, apparently the strongest state in Christendom, had been forced to yield, if not completely, at least to many of the papal demands. Excommunication, backed by brilliant opportunist diplomacy, brought similar victories in other countries (notably England, 1212), showed the Catholic church as a strong, disciplined international organization, and widely established the idea that even in its lay aspects it was answerable only to the Pope.

The Crusades had also raised Papal prestige, while the Church's bureaucracy had been continuously improved. But if great credit was gained from the first Crusade, less and less came with the later ones, and the fourth Crusade must have jolted the whole conception and subtracted from its never very great spirituality. Similarly, the growth of Papal government and its increasing need and use of money made the clergy seem worldly, even corrupt. An anti-clerical movement, drawing on the long-hidden Manicheism, significantly stressed poverty and chastity. Its many Balkan adherents were known as Bogomils; in north Italy and southern France, where they were only a little less numerous, as Catharans and Albigensians respectively. In Italy, persecution sufficed to extinguish the heresy; the Balkans were beyond the reach of the Papacy; and in France a holy war was needed. This Albigensian Crusade was a cynical plundering by freebooters (1209–29) exposing the Pope's inability to control his forces. In fact, his temporal triumphs were effected by the self-interest of men enlisted for a campaign and not by permanent forces.

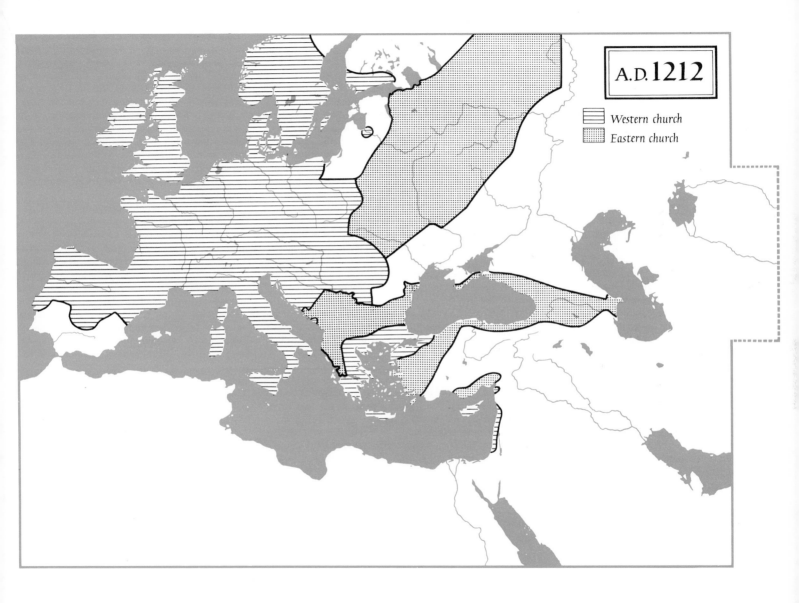

A.D.1212

⊟ Western church
⊡ Eastern church

1212 E

The inheritors of the Viking achievement were the merchants of Flanders; they brought English wool to the Flemish weaving towns and sold the finished cloth throughout the northern area. The rest of the region's trade became theirs as a result of their control of this one commodity, which increasingly dominated the rest. The Varangians lost their trade routes too, when the Cuman invasion ended Russian trade with Constantinople. The Russian principalities reorientated their exports to the Baltic and, from the twelfth century on, their tallow, honey, wax, and furs reached the West in increasing amounts. The Baltic not only carried the Russian trade, it also had fisheries richer than those in the North Sea, and fish, being an obligatory food for the medieval Christian, ranked in the northern market second only to wool. Such attractions tempted the Flemish merchants into the Baltic, but as the voyage around the Danish peninsula was a long one much traffic was transported across the base of Denmark. This shortcut brought prosperity to Lübeck, the German town at the Baltic end of the crossing,[1] a prosperity fortified by the nearby deposits of the salt, vital to the preservation of the herring catch. The German slice of the Baltic trade increased as rapidly and soon became the major one. New German towns were founded ever further east, where the ground was cleared by the pseudo-crusades of the Knights of the Sword and the Teutonic Knights. In fact the Baltic was fast becoming a German sea, when, at the beginning of the thirteenth century, Denmark burst into activity again. The Danes' valour won them a brief supremacy, but in the 1220s they suffered crippling defeat. The German towns can now be called the Hanse, for, though the Hanse were not defined until more than a century later, the association already existed and was working in pursuit of its aims – exclusion of foreign traders from the Baltic and extension of the German hegemony into the North Sea. The Flemish were in fact shut out of the Baltic by 1275 and Flemish trade declined thereafter.

Pilgrims and slaves were important commodities throughout the medieval period, particularly in the East, where slavery was much more a part of the economic system and where pilgrimage was initiated by Islam. The Western slave trade declined after the eleventh century, when the Slavs, who formed the raw material, became properly part of Christendom. But their place in trade was more than filled by the pilgrims and Crusaders of the early centuries of the second millennium; pilgrims produced a steady profit, and Crusaders, though unreliable about payment, opened up and temporarily secured the Eastern markets. Venice gathered the chief benefits, including a quarter of the Byzantine Empire – her share of the profit of the fourth Crusade. This she wisely took in the form of islands, which provided her with necessary and easily-defensible bases. The last vestiges of native enterprise were then extirpated and all commerce brought under Venetian control.

Venice's only rival was Genoa, now emerging as the dominant seaport of the western Mediterranean.[2] The two were mortal enemies, yet while they fought each other openly in the East many goods landing at Venice were passed quietly overland to Genoa for re-export to France. (Goods for Germany from Venice went over the Alps.) The Venetian creation of the Latin Empire caused Genoa to support the Byzantines and, in return, the latter granted Genoa the exemptions previously belonging to Venice.

Among Western exports to the East, woollen goods predominated. These derived only in minor degree from the northern centres, most of them being produced in north Italy, where Florence and Milan supplied the eastern and southern markets. Their increasing capacity soon outran the local wool supplies, which had to be got from as far as England. By the twelfth century, silk production had begun in northern Italy. All the large towns had a wide range of supplementary manufactures, particularly Milan, famous for its metalwork. In the booming cities of Italy Western capitalism was reborn and a full money economy revived. The use of coinage spread to the country as the urban population demanded more grain and wealthy merchants bought estates. The feudal system disintegrated.

Besides wool, manufactures, and metals, the East imported timber and timber products – pitch, tar, turpentine, and potash (potash was the most important source of alkali and was used in glass and soap manufacture, glazing, and the finishing of cloth). The East exported high-quality textiles – silks and brocades – as well as carpets, tapestries, and fruits. But the balance always depended on spices, which were, to the Near East, largely a transit trade. With troubled times overtaking the Caliphate in Mesopotamia, most of the spices came west via Egypt, whose wealth increased rapidly.

1. In the early thirteenth century much of Lübeck's growth was in the future, and its size at this date does not allow its inclusion among the towns on this map. It appears in Map 1478E, but Hamburg, at the North Sea end of the route, though wealthy, never grows sufficiently to earn this distinction.

2. Amalfi had first been the most prominent (ninth–tenth centuries). Pisa replaced her in the eleventh century, though only after Amalfi had fallen to the Normans (1131) did the Pisans finally ruin her. This was the peak of Pisan power; by the end of the twelfth century she was yielding the first place to Genoa.

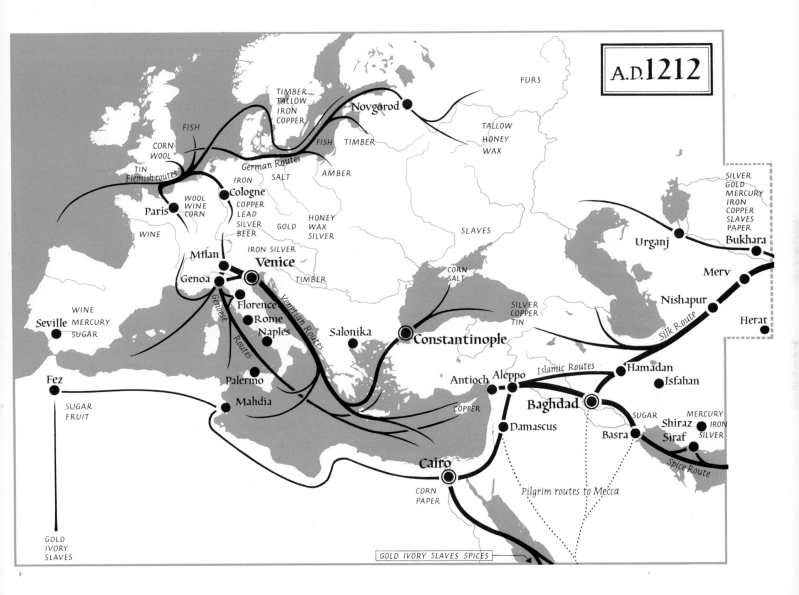

A.D. 1212

FURS

TIMBER
TALLOW
IRON
COPPER

Novgorod

TALLOW
HONEY
WAX

FISH

CORN
WOOL

FISH   TIMBER

German Routes

Flemish routes

TIN

SALT   AMBER

Paris

WINE

WOOL
WINE
CORN

Cologne

IRON
COPPER
LEAD
SILVER
BEER

GOLD

HONEY
WAX
SILVER

SLAVES

SILVER
GOLD
MERCURY
IRON
COPPER
SLAVES
PAPER

IRON SILVER

Milan

Venice

TIMBER

Urganj

Bukhara

Merv

Genoa

Genoese Routes

Venetian Routes

Florence

Rome

Naples

Salonika

CORN
SALT

Constantinople

SILVER
COPPER
TIN

Nishapur

Herat

Silk Route

Seville

WINE
MERCURY
SUGAR

Antioch   Aleppo

Islamic Routes

Hamadan

Isfahan

Fez

SUGAR
FRUIT

Palermo

Mahdia

COPPER

Damascus

Baghdad

SUGAR

Shiraz
Siraf

Basra

MERCURY
IRON
SILVER

Spice Route

Cairo

CORN
PAPER

Pilgrim routes to Mecca

GOLD
IVORY
SLAVES

GOLD IVORY SLAVES SPICES

1230

The steady rumble of medieval Mongolian history was too distant to be heard by Western ears and, though an occasional grand eruption sent whole peoples flying across the map, by the time these finally came to rest they had lost contact with their place of origin which remained outside the bounds of Western knowledge. Then, at the beginning of the thirteenth century, a new power came into being in Mongolia, one great enough to strike at either China or Europe without shifting its centre. This was the creation of the Mongol chieftain Temujin, who fused the warring nomad tribes into an invincible weapon. The council of 1206 celebrated the completion of this, the first part of his plan; the second, the conquest of the world beyond Mongolia, was there initiated, while, in anticipation, Temujin took the title of Genghis Khan, lord of the earth. By any standards except his own he can be called a successful man, for in the last twenty years of his life he made a good start towards the conquest of China, annexed the Kara Khitai Khanate, and in two merciless campaigns (1220 and 1221) smashed the Khwarizm Shahdom. During the latter war, he detached a corps to reconnoitre further westwards which delivered a series of crushing defeats to the Georgians, Alans, Cumans, and south-Russian princes (1221–2). Death came to the Khan (1227) before he could exploit the weaknesses this victorious raid disclosed. His Empire, which continued undivided, stretched from Persia to Korea; his incomparable pagan armies remained a threat to Christendom and Islam alike.

In the unconquered western fragments of the Shahdom, Khwarizmenian rule was surprisingly rapidly revived by an energetic young Shah, and though he could not challenge the Mongols he to some degree recouped himself for his father's losses by seizing Azerbaijan and Georgia. Seljuk and Ayyubid combined, however, to oppose his further advance and he fell back defeated to rest against the teeth of the Mongolian dragon. The Ayyubids let the Christians have Jerusalem and a corridor to the coast to forestall any pin-pricking Crusades while these important events marched in the East, a true if insulting assessment of the Crusader's residual potential.

Inflicted by the confederate Christians under the banner of Castile, the ruinous defeat of the Muwahids at Los Navos de Tolosa (1212) spelt the end of Moslem Spain. Leon and Castile, united from 1223, moved steadily forward thereafter. Portugal, a kingdom since 1139, quickly occupied the segment allotted to it, and Aragon, in addition to mainland advances, used the sea power of Barcelona to conquer the Balearics (1228–32).

The scramble for the Baltic lands continued: Denmark took Estonia (1230), and when the Principality of Novgorod seized Karelia (1220) the Russians came into contact with the Swedes in Finland. The German Crusaders, the Knights of the Sword, advanced up the Dvina, while a sister group, the Teutonic Knights, received permission from Poland and the Pope to start 'missionary' activities among the Prussians.

The German Empire itself was largely abandoned by its new Emperor, Frederick II Hohenstaufen, whose reign was spent trying to subdue north Italy. Officially he was reinstating the Imperial authority, but in fact he was extending the frontiers of the Kingdom of Sicily, which he had inherited and which provided the reality of his power.

The Empire of Nicaea eliminated the Latins from Asia and absorbed the Despotate of Rhodes; but the Despotate of Epirus seemed to be winning the race to Constantinople, taking Salonika in 1223 and renaming itself an Empire in celebration. The third Greek state, the Empire of Trebizond, was cut off from the others when its western half was overrun by the Seljuks (1214).

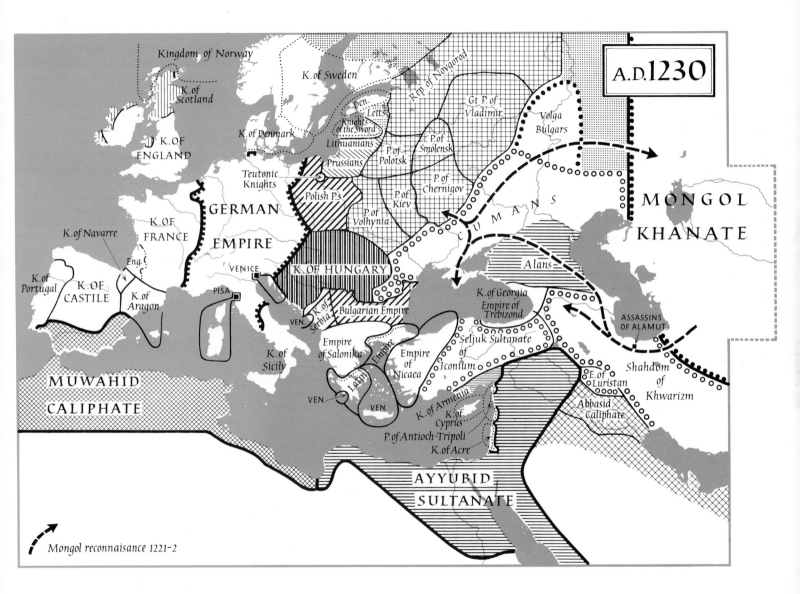

Kingdom of Norway

K. of Sweden

K. of Scotland

Rep. of Novgorod

Den.
Letts
Knights of the Sword
Lithuanians
Prussians

K. of Denmark

Gt P. of Vladimir

Volga Bulgars

MONGOL KHANATE

A.D. 1230

K. OF ENGLAND

Teutonic Knights

P. of Polotsk

P. of Smolensk

P. of Chernigov

K. of Navarre

GERMAN EMPIRE

Polish P.s

P. of Kiev

K. OF FRANCE

P. of Volhynia

C U M A N S

Eng.

K. of Portugal

K. OF CASTILE

K. of Aragon

VENICE

K. OF HUNGARY

Alans

K. of Georgia
Empire of Trebizond

ASSASSINS OF ALAMUT

PISA

VEN.

K. of Serbia

Bulgarian Empire

Seljuk Sultanate of Iconium

Shahdom of Khwarizm

K. of Sicily

Empire of Salonika

Latin Empire

Empire of Nicaea

VEN.

MUWAHID CALIPHATE

VEN.

K. of Armenia

E. of Luristan

K. of Cyprus

Abbasid Caliphate

P. of Antioch-Tripoli

K. of Acre

AYYUBID SULTANATE

▶ Mongol reconnaisance 1221-2

1278

Fifteen years elapsed between the Mongols' reconnoitring campaign of 1221–2 and their return in 1236, but no united front had been formed against them and they eliminated their opponents in orderly sequence. The Volga Bulgars (1237), the great Principality of Vladimir (1238), the Cumans and Alans (1239), and the south-Russian principalities (1240) were overrun without check. The Mongol army then split in two to invade Europe proper (1241–2). The northern force beat the Poles and the Teutonic Knights, the southern the Hungarians; but no permanent conquest was made, as the Mongols withdrew when their Khan died. It is un-Marxist to suppose that a merely human event some three and a half thousand miles away could influence the inexorable progress of history, and it is unlikely that the Mongols had the resources to impose the Tartar yoke further west than Russia for any length of time. Most of us bourgeois, however, feel that the Khan's demise saved central Europe from a very nasty ravage.

The south-Russian Principalities had been completely destroyed, and the northern Principalities, though still intact, were threatened by enemies other than their Mongol overlords. The victories of Alexander Nevsky, Prince of Novgorod, over the Swedes (1240) and the Teutonic Knights (1242) preserved the north's identity, though its freedom was to remain in pawn to the Mongols for two centuries. The north-west Russians found protectors in the Lithuanians, who alone in the Baltic succeeded in resisting the Teutonic Knights, into whose organization the Knights of the Sword had been absorbed (1237).

The Mongol advance from Persia was a series of small steps. The resurrected Khwarizm Shahdom was extinguished in 1231, Georgia conquered in 1239, and the Seljuks defeated and forced into vassaldom in 1243. (The Kingdom of Armenia and the Empire of Trebizond, Seljuk vassals for a decade, thus changed masters.) The last westward campaign opened with the extirpation of the Assassins of Alamut, which effectively ended their history (1256); its climax, the savage destruction of the Abbasid Caliphate (1258), rocked Islam; its close, the battle of Goliath's Spring (1260), marked the end of Mongol expansion. There the Mamluks, sovereigns created from among themselves by the Turkish palace guard of the last Ayyubids, defeated the Mongol attempt to seize Palestine. In the same year, the Mongol Empire was divided among the Genghis Khanid princes, only nominal supremacy remaining to Kublai, Khan of China. The relations between the western Khanates of Russia,[1] Persia, and Turkestan were never cordial and often they were at open war; with the Khanate of Persia thus distracted, the Mamluks could eliminate the Crusader cities which the less militant Ayyubids had tolerated. Jerusalem had already fallen to a horde of Khwarizmians fleeing from the Mongols (1244); the Mamluks reduced Antioch (1263), Tripoli (1289), and finally Acre (1291).

Frederick II's struggle to unify Italy was continued by his bastard heir Manfred (simply King of Sicily, not Emperor of Germany like Frederick) who found himself similarly at enmity with the Pope, a Prince of central Italy in his own right[2] and much against any Italian autocracy except his own. The Pope financed the King of France's brother, Charles of Anjou, in an attack on Manfred which succeeded (1266) so well that Charles, enfeoffed by his brother with Anjou, married to Provence and master of the Kingdom of Sicily, himself seemed the demon he had exorcized. When many of the strife-weary north-Italian cities (and Rome) surrendered to him their exhausted freedom, Charles' further progress seemed inevitable; but his ambition was too all-embracing to allow him to reshape Italy, and the north was incorrigibly particularist. Two old Norman projects absorbed much of his energy. To obtain an African province, he diverted his brother's Crusade of 1272 against Tunisia, gaining however only a temporary tribute; while eastward, by invasion (1271) and by purchasing the remnants of the Latin Empire in Greece (1278), he threatened the newly re-established Byzantines. The Empire of Nicaea had retaken Constantinople in 1261 (the Empire of Salonika had been humbled by the Bulgars in 1230 and shrank back into Epirus before the Nicaeans, who crowned their success by gaining a slice of Greece (1262)), but this final display of Byzantine resilience was only the partial success of a minor state. There was little left to face new dangers with. Fortunately for Byzantium Charles was distracted by the Sicilian revolt (1282), which occupied him for the rest of his life.

The Muwahid Caliphate disappeared in 1269, overthrown by the Marinid Sultan of Fez; it had already lost most of Spain, the little that remained becoming the independent Emirate of Granada, while on the African mainland it had been largely replaced by the Hafsids of Tunis (from 1231). The latter took the title of Caliph in 1259 on the extinction of the Baghdad Caliphate.

England brought the Welsh to heel after a final flare-up with the reorganized (1258) Principality of Wales, though the latter existed until 1282. The Scots took the isles from Norway in 1263. The Kingdom of Navarre came under French rule between 1234 and 1316.

1. The Russian Khanate was divided between the White and Golden Hordes and a third which takes its name from its first Khan, Cheiban. The Khans of Persia adopted Islam in 1295 after flirting with Nestorian Christianity. The Khans of Russia and Turkestan followed suit c. 1340.

2. His lands in central Italy were formally recognized as an independent state outside the Empire in 1278.

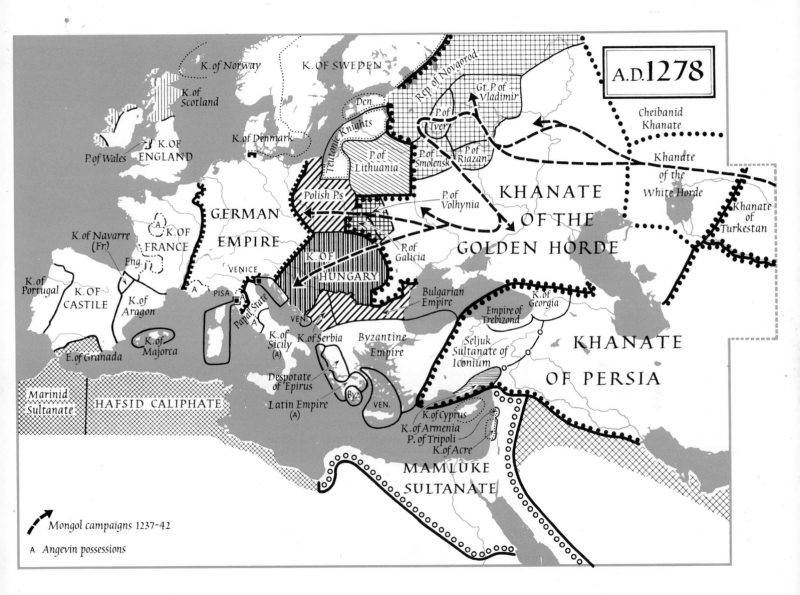

K. of Norway

K. OF SWEDEN

K. of Scotland

Rep. of Novgorod

Cheibanid Khanate

A.D. 1278

Den.

Teutonic Knights

Gt. P. of Vladimir

Khanate of the White Horde

P. of Wales

K. OF ENGLAND

K. of Denmark

P. of Tver

P. of Smolensk

P. of Riazan

P. of Lithuania

Khanate of Turkestan

Polish P.s

P. of Volhynia

KHANATE OF THE

GERMAN EMPIRE

K. of Navarre (Fr.)

(A) K. OF FRANCE

P. of Galicia

GOLDEN HORDE

Eng.

K. OF HUNGARY

K. of Portugal

K. OF CASTILE

K. of Aragon

VENICE

PISA

(A)

Papal State

Bulgarian Empire

Empire of Trebizond

K. of Georgia

KHANATE

E. of Granada

K. of Majorca

A

(A)

VEN.

K. of Sicily (A)

K. of Serbia

Byzantine Empire

Seljuk Sultanate of Iconium

OF PERSIA

Marinid Sultanate

HAFSID CALIPHATE

Despote of Epirus

Latin Empire (A)

Byz.

VEN.

K. of Cyprus

K. of Armenia

P. of Tripoli

K. of Acre

MAMLUKE SULTANATE

Mongol campaigns 1237-42

A   Angevin possessions

1360

Although the interval between this map and the last is one of the longest in the series, few major changes occurred during this period. The most striking is the disappearance of the Khanate of Persia and its client Seljuk sultanate of Iconium. They were replaced by a plethora of petty states: in Anatolia, Turkish Emirates, in eastern Persia, native provincial governments, while the diminished central power devolved on the Mongol dynasty of the Jalayrids. Of the Anatolian Emirs, the Karamanian was at first the strongest; then the gradual but inexorable conquest of Byzantine Asia altered the balance of power, for while the south-west was split between six Emirs, the entire north-west was taken by a newly arrived clan, the Ottoman.

In Europe too, Byzantine dominion withered. Its last strength was squandered in a civil war, which abandoned the recently annexed Despotate of Epirus, together with all Macedonia, to the Serbs. Under Steven Dushan, the south Slavs at last achieved an Empire, and the moment had come for them to claim the heritage of Byzantium. But Dushan's feverish attempt to reproduce in a decade of victory the splendour of a millennial decline failed for the lack of the one success that might have cemented the others: the taking of Constantinople. He died (1355) before he could attempt the siege and his Empire fell into half a dozen warring principalities; two years previously, the Ottomans had crossed to Europe and seized Gallipoli.

Nourished by Aragon (from whose royal house it drew its kings, but with which it was only briefly (1291–5) united), rebellious Sicily, on which Charles of Anjou's dreams had first come to wreck, maintained itself against attempts at reconquest that were persisted in for a century and which finally exhausted both contestants. Thereafter the Angevin course was downhill. Anjou

78

itself early became a daughter's dowry (1290), the north-Italian power, undermined by a jealous Papacy, was soon repudiated by the fractious communities, while the foothold in Serbia was lost in 1360. The Angevin dominions were thus reduced to Provence, the mainland portion of the Kingdom of Sicily (better called the Kingdom of Naples), and the Latin Empire in the Balkans, of which half – the Duchy of Athens – had been lost (1311) to a band of freebooting Aragonese. Her capacity to thwart the Angevins and the range at which she could do so is a measure of the rising power of Aragon. She profited also from the ruinous overthrow of Pisa by Genoa (1284), seizing Sardinia (1323) while Genoa took Corsica.

To offset these losses there was only the seating of an Angevin on the throne of Hungary. This Hungarian line produced in Louis the Great a true echo of Charles: brilliant, endlessly ambitious, and superficially successful. He expelled the Venetians from Dalmatia (1358), expanded at the expense of the Wallachians,[1] Serbs, and Bulgars (1365–9), and in 1370 added the crown of Poland[2] to that of Hungary. Yet in all this, he did little to increase the reality of his power and made the elementary mistake of leaving only daughters to succeed him.

Between the Marinids of Morocco and the Hafsids of Tunisia there was endless senseless strife, particularly as to who should receive the homage of the intervening Ziyanids of Algeria. In 1360, the latter were independent and the Hafsid dominion divided.

1. The Latin-speaking Wallachians and Moldavians, inhabiting modern Rumania, are first mentioned at the beginning of the fourteenth century. Their later claim to be descendants of the Roman colonists planted there in the second century A.D. seems tendentious and improbable, for the Romans' withdrawal from Rumania (270) and the appearance of the Vlach states are separated by a millennium in which the country was the property of Slav and nomad and which is devoid of all evidence of Roman survival. Almost certainly the Vlachs came from the western Balkans and only migrated into Rumania as the nomads abandoned it in the late thirteenth and early fourteenth century.

2. The Polish monarchy had been restored in 1320 after an interval of nearly two centuries.

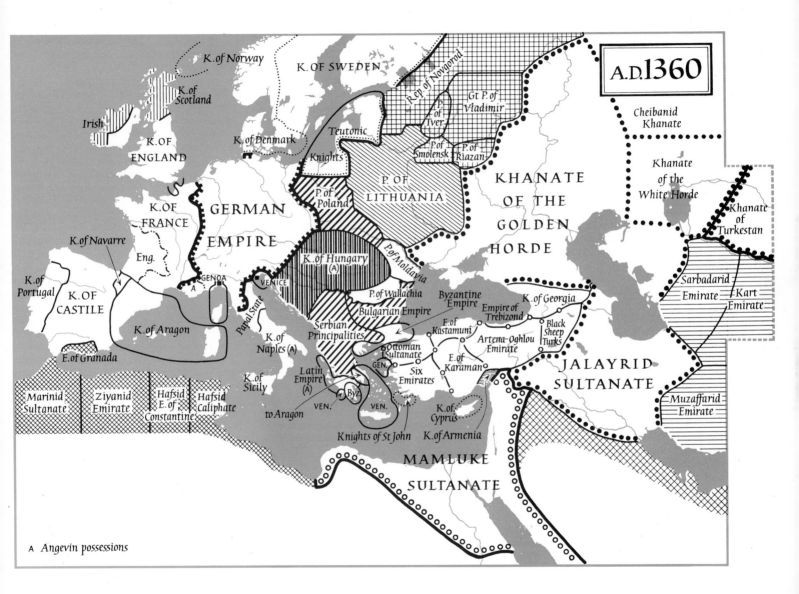

A.D. 1360

K. of Norway
K. OF SWEDEN
K. of Scotland
Irish
K. of Denmark
K. OF ENGLAND
Rep. of Novgorod
P. of Iver
Gt P. of Vladimir
Cheibanid Khanate
Teutonic Knights
P. of Smolensk
P. of Riazan
Khanate of the White Horde
P. OF LITHUANIA
K. OF FRANCE
Eng.
GERMAN EMPIRE
P. of Poland
KHANATE OF THE GOLDEN HORDE
Khanate of Turkestan
K. of Navarre
GENOA
VENICE
K. of Hungary (A)
P. of Moldavia
Sarbadarid Emirate
Kart Emirate
K. of Portugal
K. OF CASTILE
A
Papal State
K. of Aragon
K. of Naples (A)
P. of Wallachia
Byzantine Empire
Empire of Trebizond
K. of Georgia
E. of Granada
Bulgarian Empire
Serbian Principalities
E. of Kastamuni
Black Sheep Turks
Muzaffarid Emirate
K. of Sicily
Ottoman Sultanate
Artena-Oghlou Emirate
JALAYRID SULTANATE
Latin Empire (A)
GEN.
Six Emirates
E. of Karaman
Byz.
to Aragon
VEN.
VEN.
Marinid Sultanate
Ziyanid Emirate
Hafsid E. of Constantine
Hafsid Caliphate
K. of Cyprus
Knights of St John
K. of Armenia
MAMLUKE SULTANATE

A Angevin possessions

1401

In the second half of the fourteenth century, the Ottoman advance gathered speed. Attempts by the Serbs and Bulgars to dispute the Ottoman conquest of Thrace led to their defeat and Bulgaria's vassaldom (1371). Sultan Bayezid, on the first day of his reign, beat the Serbs again, this time on their home ground of Kossovo (1389). Serbia, in her turn, became a vassal of the Turks, as did Bosnia and Wallachia in 1391, while in 1396 Bulgaria was annexed outright. Resounding though these victories of Bayezid were, they were surpassed by his Asian campaigns (1390, 1392, and 1393), in which he annexed the seven remaining Anatolian Emirates (one had already been absorbed by his father in 1382). These established his eastern frontier on the Euphrates and earned him the epithet 'Thunderbolt'. Bayezid was a great warrior; it was his misfortune to encounter a greater.

Of the daughters of Louis the Great, one, with Hungary as her dowry, married the German Baron Sigismund; the other, heiress to Poland, united her state and person with Lithuania. Sigismund has his place in history, for he led the last Crusade, but, though the logistics of Crusading had improved (Sigismund had only to cross his frontier to fight the infidel), leadership had not, and he was lucky to escape from the disaster that befell his army at the hands of Bayezid at Nicopolis (1396). The Polish–Lithuanian link was loose; at first the two countries pulled in different directions. Lithuania, which had expanded to the Black Sea (1363), wished to exploit the decline of the Golden Horde and was ready to cede a province to the Teutonic Knights (1382) in return for a free hand in the East. To the Poles, the Baltic Germans were the paramount concern; in their opinion a united Poland and Lithuania would be needed to meet the German menace. When the Lithuanian attack was defeated by the Golden Horde (1399) and

80

the Black Sea outlet lost, it was to the union's profit. The dynastic merger of Norway, Sweden, and Denmark (1389, formalized 1397) was equally a response to German aggression in the Baltic.

The least glorious, though the longest lived, of the Khanates resulting from the partition of Genghis Khan's Empire was that of Turkestan. In 1363 a Turkish noble, Timur (Tamburlane) succeeded in expelling the Khan from Transoxiana; though in deference to the popular reverence for the Mongol house, he maintained a puppet Genghis Khanid as his mouthpiece. From Transoxiana, Timur led his army on repeated, devastating forays against his neighbours. Persia and Mesopotamia, in spite of continual revolts, were forced to submit after twenty years of war and massacre, but these were the only lands Timur incorporated in his Empire. His other expeditions sought plunder and fame, and earned him both in unparalleled amount. He humbled the Indian Sultans (1398–9), the Khans of Turkestan (1370, 1374, 1383, and 1389) and of the Golden Horde (1387, 1389, and 1395), and the Mamluks (1402), but never prevented his victims from rebuilding their shattered states. Timur's military capacity and his political sterility were shown in his complete overthrow of Bayezid at Ankara (1402), after which he simply reinstated the seven Anatolian Emirs, putting the Ottomans back where Bayezid had started from. (The battle incidentally saved the Byzantine Empire, reduced to Constantinople, Salonica, and an enclave in the Peloponnesus, from the inevitable result of an onslaught Bayezid had already begun.) As a great captain, Timur perhaps outshone Genghis Khan. Before his onslaught, the Ottomans were triumphant, the Mamluks vigorous (they conquered Armenia in 1375) and the Golden Horde[1] still formidable (they sacked rebellious Moscow, capital of the Principality of Vladimir[2] in 1382). Damas-

cus, Brusa, Sarai, and Delhi were the metropoli of the Islamic powers, and it is curious that the fanatical Moslem Timur sacked all these and yet could injure the hated infidel only by terrorizing the miniscule Kingdom of Georgia (1394, 1399, 1400, 1403).

Since the twelfth century the French had been edging forward on the southern half of their frontier with the German Empire. By the first decade of the fourteenth the right bank of the lower Rhône was wholly French, and some French fiefs lay across the river. They were soon augmented, principally in 1385, when Provence was seized at the instigation of the Avignon Pope, who had been refused recognition by the Neapolitan Angevins during the papal schism. This brought the border to the Alps, and when Genoa, reeling from her final defeat by Venice, accepted French protection (1396), the stage seemed set for full-scale French intervention in Italy. But that was to be delayed another century; the protectorate was repudiated by Genoa in 1409. In south-west France the extent of the English estates fluctuated, but in spite of fine English victories they tended to dwindle. However, the gains of the French monarchy were offset by the continual endowment of the King's brothers with extensive duchies. That of Burgundy plus land in Germany went to one who later married the heiress of wealthy Flanders and thus came to rank as a European power. In Albania, Western adventurers founded petty states later swept away by the Turkish flood.

1. In 1380 the Golden Horde was conquered by the White, which then migrated into its territories. The Khanate continued to be known in the West as the Golden Horde.

2. The town of Vladimir never recovered from the sack by the Mongols in 1237, but the title of Great Prince of Vladimir remained the seal of leadership in north-east Russia. It was competed for by the previously minor Princes of Moscow and Tver, with Moscow usually successful.

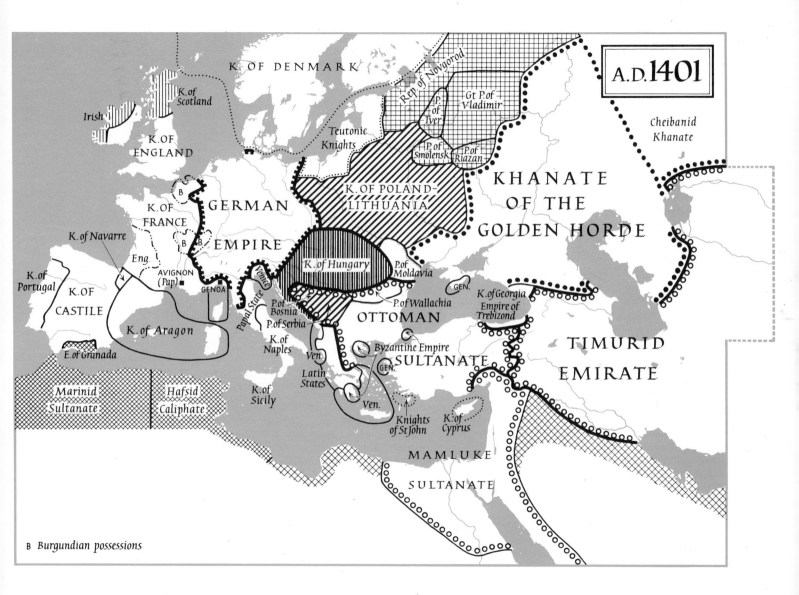

K. OF DENMARK

K. of
Scotland

Irish

K. OF
ENGLAND

Rep. of Novgorod

Gt P. of
Vladimir

P. of
Tver

A.D. 1401

Cheibanid
Khanate

Teutonic
Knights

P. of
Smolensk

P. of
Riazan

K. OF POLAND-
LITHUANIA

KHANATE
OF THE
GOLDEN HORDE

GERMAN

K. of Navarre

K. OF
FRANCE

B

B

Eng.

AVIGNON
(Pap.)

B

EMPIRE

K. of Hungary

P. of
Moldavia

K. of
Portugal

K. OF
CASTILE

GENOA

Venice

Papal State

P. of
Bosnia
P. of Serbia

P. of Wallachia

GEN.

K. of Georgia
Empire of
Trebizond

K. of Aragon

K. of
Naples

OTTOMAN

SULTANATE

TIMURID

EMIRATE

E. of Granada

Ven.

Byzantine Empire

GEN.

Marinid
Sultanate

Hafsid
Caliphate

K. of Sicily

Latin
States

Ven.

Knights
of St John

K. of
Cyprus

MAMLUKE

SULTANATE

B Burgundian possessions

1430

When Henry the Fifth invaded France he was not trying to regain the lost English fiefs, he was attempting to seize the French throne. Alliance with the separatist and ambitious Duke of Burgundy, already inclined to England by the mutual traffic in wool, gave a solid base on which Henry's military skill could build. Agincourt (1415) won the whole north and the promise of the crown, but the legitimate heir refused to recognize this surrender and set up an opposition government south of the Loire. In 1429 came Joan of Arc and the turn of the tide, the English quickly losing Champagne (the part of France between Burgundy proper and the Burgundian possessions in the Low Countries). The Duke of Burgundy now held the balance of power between the two main contestants, and when in 1435 he transferred his support to France, in return for autonomy, the expulsion of the English became only a matter of time.

Two hundred years of struggle between German, Slav, and Balt culminated in the battle of Tannenberg (1411), where the Teutonic Knights were vanquished by the Polish–Lithuanian army. The Knights had, however, monopolized the sympathy of the West, which saw them as selfless crusaders in a heathen land – a view which would have been merely naïve when applied to the original efforts of the Knights, but which was quite absurd at the beginning of the fifteenth century. Diplomatic pressure was put on the exhausted victors, who accepted a peace by which only the most recently usurped province was regained.

The collapse of the Ottomans following the battle of Ankara offered the Christians a unique opportunity for expelling the Moslems from the Balkans. The Anatolian half of the Ottoman Empire all but disappeared, and, as the sons of Bayezid squabbled over the European remainder, Bosnia and Serbia found themselves free again.

By contrast, Christendom appeared to gain in unity when Sigismund of Hungary became German Emperor (1410) and then King of Bohemia (1419), but the power that his titles suggest never in fact materialized. The Empire was oblivious of its Emperor's existence; Bohemia in glorious revolt (1419–36); and Hungary itself, torn by civil wars, at such a low ebb that Venice was able to regain the Dalmatian coast. So nothing was done to prevent the reconstitution of the Ottoman nucleus, which between 1426 and 1428 demonstrated its recovery by annexing five of the Anatolian emirates re-erected by Timur. The Ottoman advance in Europe started up again with the conquest of Albania and Salonika (1430); the moment for Christian counter-attack had been lost.

Considering that Timur had ignored every instrument of government except terror, it is remarkable that his immediate successors managed to retain control of most of his empire. The western part of Persia was lost to the Black Sheep Turks (1408), whose power consequently eclipsed that of their rivals, the White Sheep Turks, whom Timur had set up against them in Anatolia. Two years later, the Black Sheep Turks seized Mesopotamia, putting an end to the Jalayrid sultanate which had been re-established there in 1405. Then, Turk and Timurid balanced against each other, an uneasy peace descended on the devastated land.

With the reconquest of Spain still incomplete, the Christians began the counter-invasion of Morocco, the Portuguese seizing Ceuta in 1415. The decline of the Moroccan Marinids, which this feat made apparent, opened the way for the Hafsids to gain a titular supremacy over the whole of western North Africa.

Sicily was united to its parent kingdom in 1409. Smolensk was absorbed by Poland–Lithuania in 1404. The Crimean Turks split off from the declining Golden Horde (1430).

Ireland, which had been slipping from the English grip for over a century, finally drifted back to its aboriginally squalid freedom.

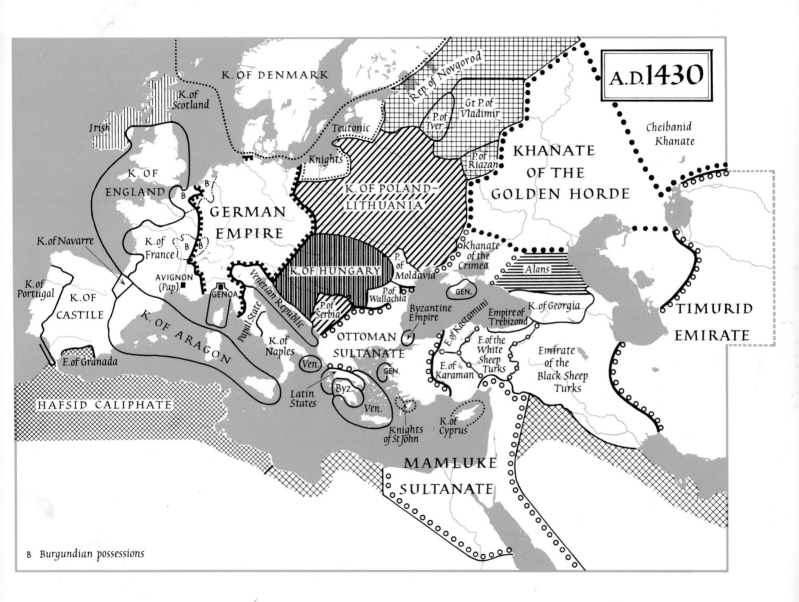

K. OF DENMARK

K. of Scotland

Irish

Rep. of Novgorod

Gt P. of Vladimir

Cheibanid Khanate

P. of Tver

Teutonic

Knights

P. of Riazan

KHANATE OF THE GOLDEN HORDE

K. OF ENGLAND

B

GERMAN EMPIRE

K. OF POLAND-LITHUANIA

K. of Navarre

K. of France

S B B

Khanate of the Crimea

Alans

AVIGNON (Pap)

P. of Moldavia

K. OF HUNGARY

TIMURID EMIRATE

K. of Portugal

K. OF CASTILE

GENOA

Papal State

Venetian Republic

P. of Wallachia

GEN.

K. OF ARAGON

K. of Naples

P. of Serbia

Byzantine Empire

K. of Georgia

E. of Kastamuni

Empire of Trebizond

E. of Granada

Ven.

OTTOMAN SULTANATE

GEN.

E. of the White Sheep Turks

HAFSID CALIPHATE

Latin States

Byz.

Ven.

E. of Karaman

Emirate of the Black Sheep Turks

Knights of St John

K. of Cyprus

MAMLUKE SULTANATE

A.D. 1430

B Burgundian possessions

1478

If the Duke of Burgundy took pride in ruling the wealthiest state in Europe, he also fretted at its division. By war and purchase the last Duke opened a corridor between the Low Countries and Burgundy proper, but then became embroiled with the Swiss at the southern end of his dominions and unexpectedly suffered a series of defeats, culminating in his death and the final ruin of his cause at the battle of Nancy (1477). Since Adrianople, cavalry had had their ups and downs, but had always been necessary for victory and by and large had dominated the battlefield. The slaughter of the Burgundian knights by the Swiss pike-men brought infantry to the fore again and showed that unsupported foot could win the day. France leapt into action after Burgundy's disaster, determined to eliminate forever the vassal that had humiliated her so often, but though King Louis XI moved rapidly the heiress of Burgundy preserved almost all of the Netherlands and Flanders by marrying the head of the Hapsburg house and enlisting his aid. The Hapsburgs had already made themselves the most powerful of the German barons (after 1438 the German crown was always bestowed on a Hapsburg); for them the acquisition of the Low Countries was but the start of a genealogical joyride that was to culminate fifty years later in the Hapsburg Charles the Fifth, Emperor of Germany, master of Castile, Aragon, Navarre, Sardinia, Sicily, Naples, Flanders, the Netherlands, and more. In 1478 it would have been difficult to imagine such an estate, for Spain was still much divided and, though Aragon had conquered Naples in 1442, in 1458 it was again made a separate kingdom, this time for a royal bastard. The union of Aragon and Castile by the famous marriage of Ferdinand and Isabella and the reversion of the Kingdom of Naples were to provide the daughter whose dowry was the Hapsburg jackpot.

The English were finally expelled from France (except Calais) in 1453; Scotland received the Orkneys and Shetlands from Denmark in 1472; and Sweden left the Scandinavian union in 1448. Stability was finally coming to the map of Western Europe, which was to continue much the same until the nineteenth century. Eastern Europe was another matter, though the refusal of the great Prince of Moscow (the archaic title of Vladimir can now be dropped) to pay tribute to the moribund Golden Horde and his conquest of Novgorod (1478) prefigured the Muscovite domination of Russia. Independent isolated Tver was not to see the end of the century; Pskov, which had saved itself by betraying its parent Novgorod, and Riazan, were to be absorbed in the opening decades of the next, by which time the long task of rolling back the Polish Kingdom had begun. Poland, though rewarded with overwhelming success in the last struggle with the Teutonic Knights (1466), showed a flabbiness in failing to secure their final elimination that betokened weakness, and was later to be slowly squashed between German and Russian. The fifteenth century was the apogee of the Polish state; Lithuania was properly part of it after 1430, while Moldavia was a vassal, and Bohemia, in the high tide of a Slav reaction, an appendage of the Polish crown (Moravia and Lusatia, the other Slav parts of the German Empire, went to Hungary). Briefly (1439–44) Hungary too had been united with Poland, producing one of those unreal agglomerations typical of the times. If they were in reply to the Turkish threat, they were ineffective, for, as Sigismund had discovered, war against the infidel needed armies, and a collection of crowns in itself produced little more than social éclat. Christendom's failure to respond significantly to the Ottoman advance was perhaps a failure to see what was at stake. Crusading had an unfortunate emotional aura that had been responsible for many disasters and the little consequence that these had had for the West underlined the impression that Crusading was unnecessary as well as impractical. It was only with the fall of Constantinople (1453) that the reality and magnitude of the Christian loss became apparent. The Byzantine Empire had long before shrivelled away and its demise was overdue; in such a context the final sack might have come as an anticlimax. But Constantinople, even the dried husk of it, outweighed any other city, and its gates were the gates of the East. When the few thousand defenders had been overwhelmed and the Turk stormed in triumph through streets that had been deserted generations before, the West, shut out of the Eastern routes it had hitherto monopolized, saw itself deprived of half its heritage. The fourth Crusade had come home to roost.

The other Ottoman conquests can be briefly listed: in Europe – Serbia (1439), Southern Greece (1456–8), Bosnia (1463), Wallachia (1475); in Asia Minor – the remaining two Emirates and the pathetic little Empire of Trebizond (1431–71). Events further east were to have little bearing on European history once the Ottoman barrier had been effectively erected. The White Sheep Turks vanquished their enemies of the Black Sheep in 1467 and pressed hard on the expiring Timurids, but these events have not the ring of the old Arab and Mongol conquests. The Near East was becoming a backwater. On the Russian steppe, there was the same diminuendo; discontented sections of the Golden Horde founded the minor Khanates of Kazan (1445) and Astrakhan (1466) at the expense of the main horde, already less powerful than the Crimean Khanate, which received the support and acknowledged the suzerainty of the Ottomans. The Cheibanid Khanate collapsed in 1471; the Golden Horde lasted till 1502.

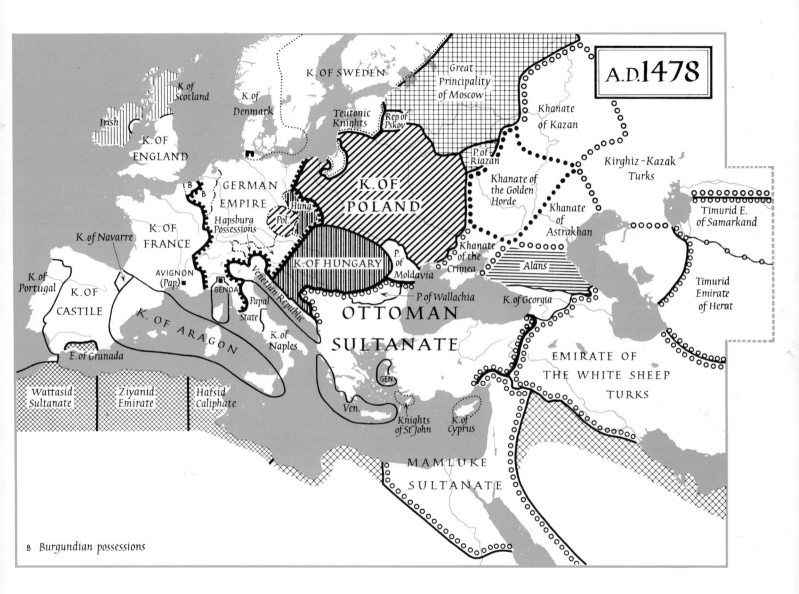

K.of Scotland

Irish

K. OF ENGLAND

K.of Denmark

K. OF SWEDEN

Great Principality of Moscow

Teutonic Knights

Rep of Pskov

Khanate of Kazan

GERMAN EMPIRE

B

Hapsburg Possessions

Hung.

Pol.

K. OF POLAND

P. of Riazan

Kirghiz-Kazak Turks

Khanate of the Golden Horde

Timurid E. of Samarkand

K. OF FRANCE

AVIGNON (Pap)

GENOA

Venetian Republic

K. OF HUNGARY

P. of Moldavia

Khanate of Astrakhan

Khanate of the Crimea

Alans

Timurid Emirate of Herat

K.of Navarre

K. OF CASTILE

K.of Portugal

K. OF ARAGON

Papal State

K. of Naples

P. of Wallachia

K.of Georgia

E. of Granada

Ven.

GEN.

OTTOMAN SULTANATE

EMIRATE OF THE WHITE SHEEP TURKS

Wattasid Sultanate

Ziyanid Emirate

Hafsid Caliphate

Knights of St John

K. of Cyprus

MAMLUKE SULTANATE

A.D.1478

B Burgundian possessions

1478 R

The medieval period is often referred to as the age of faith, and insofar as this means that, without significant exception, the inhabitants of Western continental Europe were Christian and had faith, the phrase is apt enough. In the early, pre-1000 period this faith was truly unquestioning, and there was little conflict between what the Church taught and what seemed natural in the isolated, rural communities that made up Western society. After this date, the steady advance in the economy opened a breach between everyday practice and the laws laid down by the Church, which widened the more rapidly for the clerical anathematization of all innovations, from usury to the cross bow. At the same time the special position of the clergy in respect of taxation and temporal responsibility was condemned by kings seeking to establish a real national unity in their dominions. The political blunders of the Papacy were numerous (a particularly striking one was the long-continued Papal support of the Angevins in the Sicilian war) and its crimes of corruption and nepotism were perhaps greater and certainly better publicized; but the repeated ill-success of the Popes and the steady downward trend of their prestige in the later Middle Ages were largely inevitable and only partly a consequence of their inability to adapt to the new society.

The Papal State in Italy, recognized as independent by the Emperor in 1278, was an unhappy attempt to provide a temporal basis for Papal power. To gain it much of the spiritual wealth of the Church was squandered, but the inability of the Church to rule the lands it had fought for so misguidedly allowed them to slide into lawlessness. So complete was this disintegration that in 1309 the Papacy had, for safety's sake, to withdraw to Avignon[1] in southern France, and when in 1377 a Pope did return to Rome, he was on the point of going back to Avignon again when he died. The Roman mob seized its chance and forced the College of Cardinals to elect a Pope whom they fancied would favour the permanent re-establishment of the Papacy in Rome. The Cardinals escaped as soon as they could, repudiated the Pope who had been forced upon them, and created another of their own choosing. After a scuffle, the second Pope and the Cardinals were forced to flee back to Avignon, while the first reigned in Rome, supported by a College of Cardinals entirely of his own making. Thus began the great Schism which divided the allegiance of Christendom[2] and brought the Papacy to its nadir. Thirty years later, a general council of the Church met at Pisa and attempted to restore order, but it only succeeded in adding a third Pope to the scene. The next council (held at Constance, 1414–18) managed to make the deposition of all three effective and re-established the unity of the Papacy and the outward dignity of the Church. It stalled, however, on the crucial question of reform and turned savagely on those who attempted to take matters into their own hands, burning the Bohemian, Huss, for his refusal to accept its dictates (1416). Huss had found in the renascent Slavs of Bohemia eager support for his attack on authority, and his followers after his death not only continued to stigmatize clerical corruption, but succeeded in eliminating it from the Bohemian Church. Their insistence on cleric and laity sharing alike in the Communion bridged the widening gulf between the two in defiance of the doctrinal despotism of the Pope. The faithful were consequently ordered to attack the Hussite heretics, but the Crusade was a fiasco. For twenty years (1419–39) the Bohemians lorded it over southern Germany before the hierarchy acquiesced in a compromise. By then another council had met at Basle (1431) to discuss the ever postponed reform of the Church, the need for which had been pressing for a century. The council started briskly quarrelling with the Pope as to which of the two had the ultimate authority in Christendom, and matters soon progressed to open rupture and another schism (1439–49). With such fiddling the time passed; the official reform movement collapsed and the deluge, of which the Hussites had been the herald, was rendered inevitable.

While political insignificance was fast becoming the lot of Western Christendom, political extinction overtook the Eastern Orthodox Church. As the Turks steadily whittled down the Byzantine Empire, the Byzantine Emperor saw a hope of survival in accepting the authority of Rome as the price of Western support. But the reunion of 1439 was insincere, never accepted by the people of Constantinople, and always denounced by their clergy. In any case, the days when the Papacy could direct the armaments of the West were long past, and the Emperor was soon brought to realize this. Byzantium fought and fell in the name of the Orthodox Church. Only the rising star of Muscovy and the dying glow of Georgia remained to the Orthodox as the long night of Ottoman supremacy began.

---

1. Avignon was finally purchased outright by the Papacy in 1348.

2. France, Spain (except Portugal), and Scotland supported the Pope of Avignon, a line-up which reflected current political alliances.

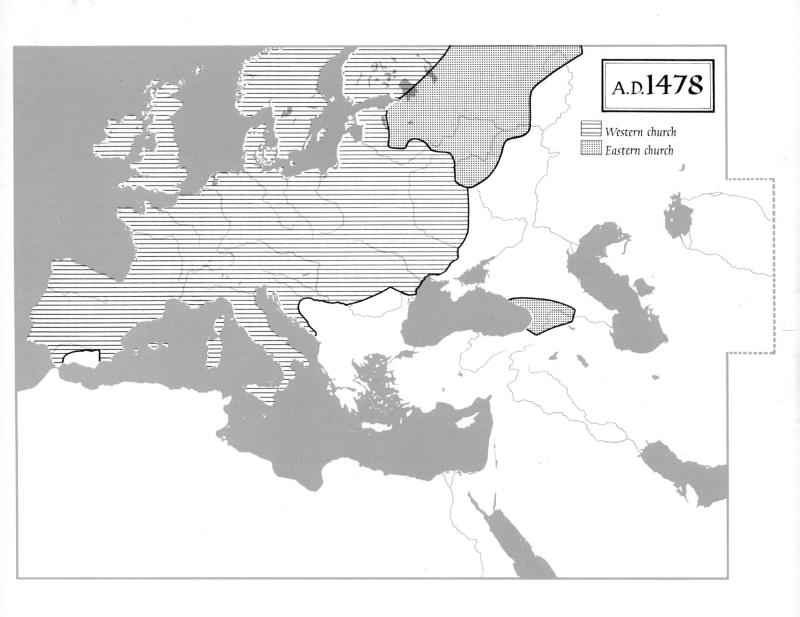

A.D.1478

Western church
Eastern church

1478 E

The growth of the West-European economy continued at a rapid rate until the middle of the fourteenth century when, for a variety of reasons, there was a levelling off, if not an actual slump. To contemporaries, it seemed obvious that this was due to the Black Death, which decimated the population, particularly in the towns, and it is still simplest to refer to the last two phases of medieval economic history as pre- and post-Black Death.

In the pre-Black Death period, the towns of the German Hanse prospered greatly and achieved an effective monopoly of the Baltic–North Sea trade. The conquests of the Teutonic Knights opened up the Baltic hinterland and the Grand Master of the Order, himself a member of the Hanse, became the greatest corn merchant in the world. From 1280 on, his grain reached the West in increasing quantity and caused a significant lowering of price. (The Grand Master also reserved to himself the right to deal in amber, the most ancient of Baltic commodities.) In return, Russia and the Baltic states principally imported textiles; generally the commodities of northern trade remained the same as in previous centuries, though by this time the first coal was being shipped from Northumberland. Both there and in the Low Countries, coal had been used locally for some time previously, but it was only in the fourteenth century that it was recognized as a valuable fuel beyond the immediate areas of its natural occurrence.

Italian production was stagnating even before the arrival of the Black Death. Italy had few raw materials and its manufacturers became increasingly tied to high quality goods. From 1300 on, Venetian and Genoese ships took these and Eastern wares directly to north Europe via the Atlantic. The ships returned with English wool and with goods for re-export to the East. Great riches still came to Italy from this East–West trade and disguised the failure to maintain a real expansion of industry. Genoa profited from the Byzantine restoration of 1261, being awarded some Aegean islands and, more important, getting control of the Black Sea. Once the Mongols had established peace in Asia, the caravan routes became busier than ever before, and, with two of the three trans-Asian routes ending at the Black Sea,[1] Genoese merchants had no illusions about the value of their hegemony in the area. Although Venice regained admittance to the Byzantine ports in the early fourteenth century, she never managed to displace Genoa in the Black Sea; elsewhere, she was always ahead, and in wealth and power Genoa never equalled her.

It was along the northernmost caravan route that the Black Death (bubonic plague) came to Europe. It spread from the Crimea (1346) via Constantinople to Italy and Western Europe (1348), then to the North Sea and Baltic countries (1350). Its immediate mortality was certainly colossal (perhaps a quarter to a third in the areas it affected) and it flared up at intervals for centuries after, but it is not necessary to suppose that its effect on the economy was purely disruptive. It can be argued that to remove a quarter of the population will cause food prices to fall as only the best land continues in use. Wages will rise because the money in circulation is constant, a simple inflationary effect, but the scarcity of labour would be likely to elicit a rise in real wages. All this sound specious, but in fact a considerable amount of evidence has been gathered to support the view that per capita the post-Black Death population was better off. However, the community as a whole was poorer and, worse than that, was left with a smaller rate of increase. To thrive, a capitalist economy must expand and the Black Death put a stop to market growth by population rise. This was the more serious in that at the same time the German colonization of the Baltic and Slav countries came to an end, while the Mongol rule in Asia collapsed and the overland trade they had encouraged fell off catastrophically. In the post-Black Death phase, the economy of the Europe–Near East area was contracted and sluggish. The Hanse assumed a defensive posture; it was, in fact, the need to hang on to the gains of earlier days that led to the Hanse being formulated as a disciplined body. A war with Denmark brought a repetition of the victory of 1227 and confirmed the Hanseatic domination of Scandinavian economy. An English challenge to their monopoly of the Baltic and North Sea proved more difficult to beat off. However, civil war distracted the English and in the end it was the Dutch who succeeded in reopening the route around the Danish peninsula. After that, the Hanse were in retreat, like their most powerful member, the Grand Master of the Teutonic Knights. Even the fish deserted the Germans; after 1420 the Baltic catch declined, while the North Sea haul, which the Hanse could not control, steadily increased in value.

In the fifteenth century, almost all salt came from deposits near the mouth of the Loire.

From 1350 on, the English made up an increasing proportion of their wool into cloth before exporting it, and the weavers of Flanders and of Italy had to fill the gap with wool of poorer quality from Spain and Ireland. However, English cloth was still sent to the Low Countries to undergo the complicated process of 'finishing', a craft of which the Dutch long remained the masters.

The disappearance of the pro-Christian Mongols and the arrival of the uncooperative Ottomans increased the risks and diminished the returns of the East–West trade. The sea routes remained fairly safe and profitable however so long as the Venetians and Genoese retained their

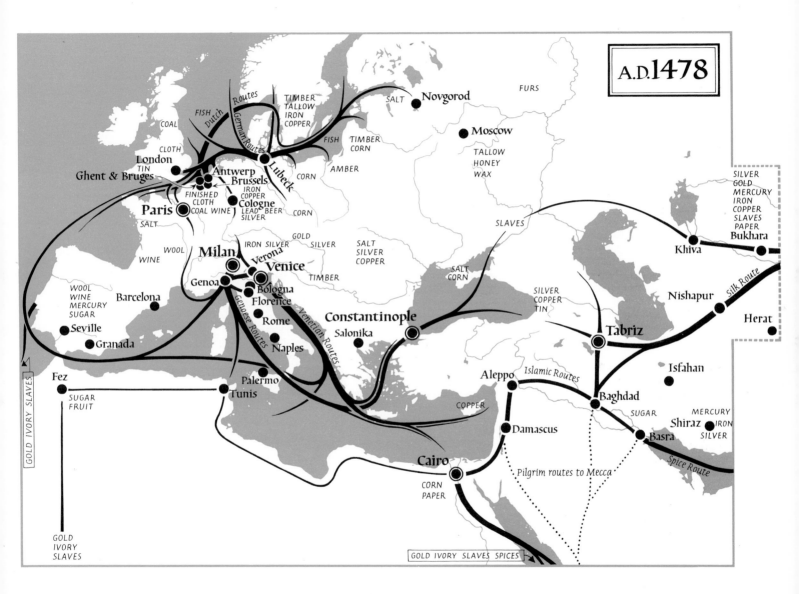

A.D. 1478

FURS

SALT — Novgorod

TIMBER
TALLOW
IRON
COPPER

Moscow

TALLOW
HONEY
WAX

Routes

Dutch

FISH

German Routes

COAL

CLOTH

London

TIN

Ghent & Bruges

Antwerp
Brussels

Lübeck

FISH

TIMBER
CORN

CORN

AMBER

SILVER
GOLD
MERCURY
IRON
COPPER
SLAVES
PAPER

FINISHED
CLOTH

IRON
COPPER

Paris

COAL WINE

Cologne

LEAD BEER
SILVER

CORN

SLAVES

Bukhara

SALT

WOOL

WINE

Milan

Verona

GOLD

SILVER

Khiva

SALT
SILVER
COPPER

WOOL
WINE
MERCURY
SUGAR

Barcelona

Genoa

IRON SILVER

Venice

SALT
CORN

Nishapur

Silk Route

Bologna
Florence

Rome

TIMBER

Venetian Routes

Constantinople

SILVER
COPPER
TIN

Tabriz

Herat

Seville

Genoese Routes

Salonika

Isfahan

Granada

Naples

Islamic Routes

Fez

Palermo

Aleppo

SUGAR
FRUIT

Tunis

COPPER

Baghdad

SUGAR

MERCURY

Damascus

Shiraz

IRON
SILVER

Basra

Spice Route

GOLD IVORY SLAVES

Cairo

Pilgrim routes to Mecca

GOLD
IVORY
SLAVES

CORN
PAPER

GOLD IVORY SLAVES SPICES

string of island bases in the East and while Constantinople held open the Turkish jaws encircling the Black Sea. Genoese and Venetians fought each other the more bitterly as the situation became more precarious and never combined to stem the advance of Islam. Their long struggle reached a bitter climax in 1379–80, when the Genoese laid siege to Venice and were overthrown. Genoa had shot her bolt and never again did Venice come so near to losing her Mediterranean supremacy. In the fifteenth century Venice annexed much of the north-Italian plain, an enterprise that safeguarded her Transalpine route to Germany and guaranteed her corn supply but involved her in the perpetual and debilitating wars of the Italian city states from which she had hitherto held aloof.

In the sphere of finance the Italian remained master until the end of the Middle Ages. The banking system reached its highest efficiency and the banks their greatest size in Italy, and it was there that the first gold coinage in the West was minted (Florence, 1252). The Papal tax-collecting organization naturally favoured Italian employees and this preference did much to establish and maintain the predominance of Italians in European banking – a predominance so marked that even the North-Sea trade was largely financed by them.

The rate of technological advance during the medieval period was desperately slow, particularly in the first half when the few discoveries that were made took literally centuries to become widely accepted. The replacement of the simple plough by the wheeled one and the use of the horse rather than the ox to draw it,[2] were processes that began in Carolingian times and remained incomplete at the end of the Middle Ages. Sometimes an invention got completely forgotten – a case in point is Greek Fire.[3]

Against such a background the innovations of the last quarter of the medieval period appear numerous and revolutionary. Gunpowder, the compass, and printing are the highlights of a trend that was discernible in the fields of mining, metallurgy, manufacturing, and navigation and that was healthily concerned with practical results. Pumps, ore crushers, and fulling and paper-manufacturing machinery were developed within the limitations imposed by the restriction of power to that obtainable from wind and waterfall. As discrepancies between the rigid dogmata of the schoolmen and the actual nature of things became increasingly apparent, the old systems of logic fell into disrepute and a theoretical science was born which asked new questions and repeatedly returned to reality to check the validity of its reasoning. Empiricism, enquiry, and theory blended in the Portuguese captains who in the fifteenth century sailed ever further south along the coast of Africa paying for their expeditions by bringing back the slaves, gold, and ivory of the western Sudan. The cape was reached and rounded in 1488 and ten years later Vasco da Gama finally reached the rich Indian market. By then the Genoese Columbus was already setting out on his third voyage to America. The walls that had confined Europe throughout the Middle Ages were shattered; the last decades of the fifteenth century during which this work was done are a part of Modern History.

1. At Trebizond and at the mouth of the Don. The last swung north of Syria which was in the hands of the Mamluks, the Mongols' deadly enemies, and reached the sea via the Kingdom of Armenia.

2. A substitution that was long held up by the lack of a collar that would enable the horse to pull without throttling itself.

3. Greek Fire is a term applied loosely to any incendiary matter used in medieval warfare, but it strictly refers to a liquid that ignited spontaneously on contact with water and which was used in naval battles. The basic material in nearly all these mixtures was petrol, which occurs on the surface in the eastern Caucasus; the secret additive that caused ignition on contact with water was certainly calcium phosphide, probably manufactured by heating a mixture of lime and bones with urine.

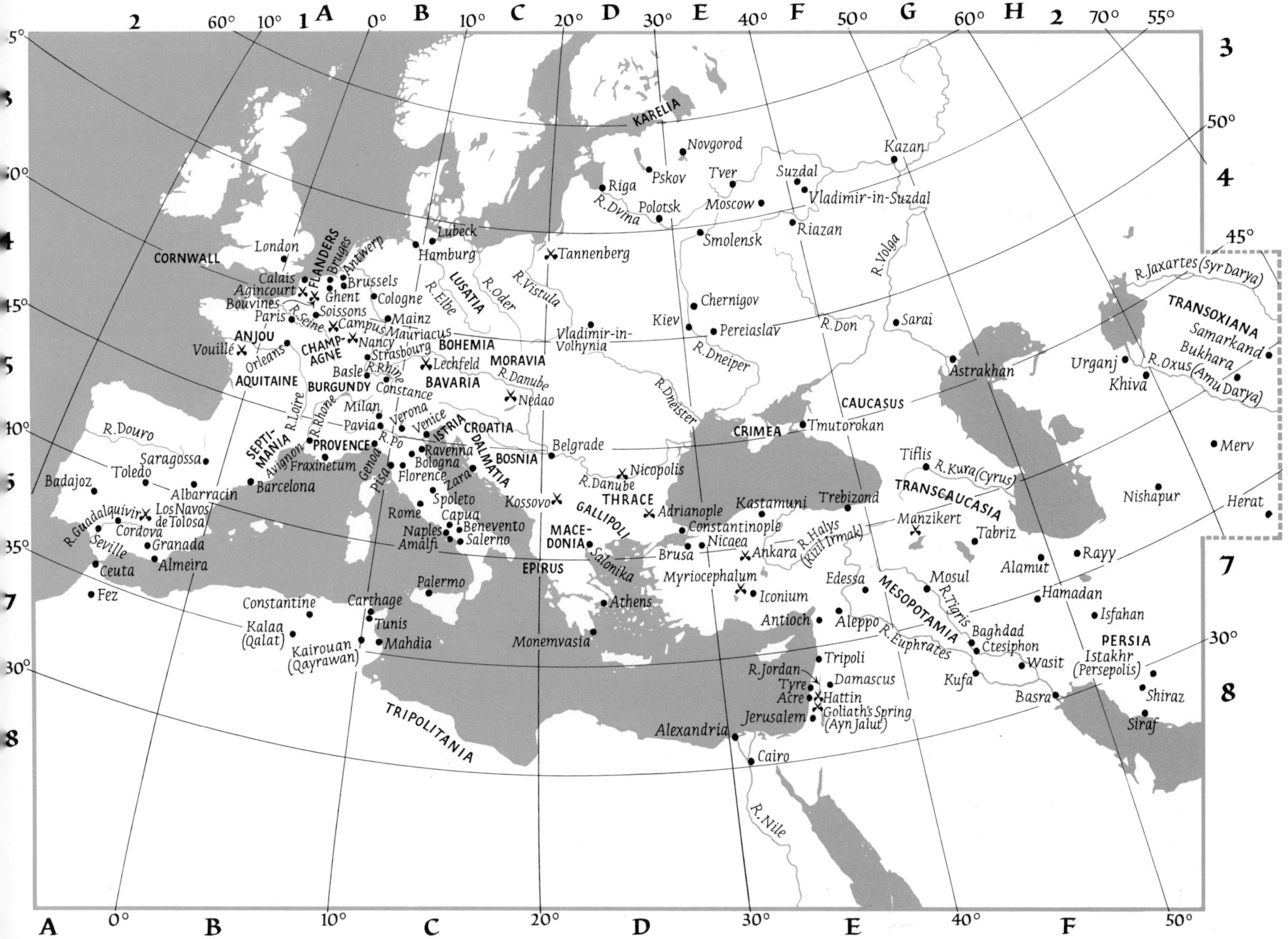
KARELIA
Novgorod
Pskov
Riga
R. Dvina
Polotsk
Tver
Moscow
Suzdal
Vladimir-in-Suzdal
Kazan
Riazan
Smolensk
R. Volga
Lubeck
Hamburg
Tannenberg
CORNWALL
London
FLANDERS
Bruges
Antwerp
Calais
Agincourt
Brussels
Ghent
Bouvines
Cologne
R. Elbe
LUSATIA
R. Oder
R. Vistula
Paris
R. Seine
Soissons
Mainz
Campus Mauriacus
ANJOU
Vouillé
Orleans
CHAMP-AGNE
Nancy
Strasbourg
BOHEMIA
MORAVIA
Lechfeld
Basle
R. Rhine
AQUITAINE
BURGUNDY
Constance
BAVARIA
R. Danube
Nedao
Vladimir-in-Volhynia
Chernigov
Kiev
Pereiaslav
R. Dneiper
R. Dniester
R. Don
Sarai
Astrakhan
R. Jaxartes (Syr Darya)
TRANSOXIANA
Samarkand
Bukhara
Urganj
Khiva
R. Oxus (Amu Darya)
R. Loire
R. Rhone
Milan
Verona
Pavia
Venice
ISTRIA
CROATIA
R. Douro
SEPTI-MANIA
PROVENCE
R. Po
Ravenna
DALMATIA
BOSNIA
Belgrade
CRIMEA
Tmutorokan
CAUCASUS
Saragossa
Avignon
Fraxinetum
Genoa
Bologna
Toledo
Pisa
Florence
Zara
Badajoz
Albarracin
Barcelona
Spoleto
Nicopolis
R. Danube
THRACE
Kossovo
Rome
Capua
Benevento
GALLIPOLI
Adrianople
Kastamuni
Trebizond
Tiflis
R. Kura (Cyrus)
TRANSCAUCASIA
Merv
Nishapur
Herat
R. Guadalquivir
Los Navos de Tolosa
Cordova
Seville
Granada
Naples
Amalfi
Salerno
MACE-DONIA
Constantinople
Nicaea
Brusa
Ankara
R. Halys (Kizil Irmak)
Manzikert
Tabriz
Rayy
Alamut
Ceuta
Almeira
Salonika
EPIRUS
Myriocephalum
Edessa
MESOPOTAMIA
Mosul
R. Tigris
Hamadan
Fez
Palermo
Constantine
Carthage
Tunis
Athens
Iconium
Antioch
Aleppo
Isfahan
Kalaa (Qalat)
Kairouan (Qayrawan)
Mahdia
Monemvasia
R. Euphrates
Baghdad
Ctesiphon
PERSIA
Wasit
Istakhr (Persepolis)
Tripoli
R. Jordan
Damascus
Tyre
Acre
Hattin
Kufa
Basra
Shiraz
Goliath's Spring (Ayn Jalut)
Jerusalem
Siraf
TRIPOLITANIA
Alexandria
Cairo
R. Nile
A
B
C
D
E
F
G
H
1
2
3
4
5
6
7
8
0°
10°
20°
30°
40°
50°
60°
70°
30°
35°
40°
45°
50°
55°
60°